INTERPERSONAL RELATIONSHIP SKILLS FOR MINISTERS

INTERPERSONAL RELATIONSHIP SKILLS FOR MINISTERS

EDITED BY
JEANINE CANNON BOZEMAN
& ARGILE SMITH

PELICAN PUBLISHING COMPANY
GRETNA 2007

First printing, October 2004
Second printing, December 2007

Library of Congress Cataloging-in-Publication Data

Interpersonal relationship skills for ministers / edited by Jeanine
Cannon Bozeman and Argile Smith.
  p. cm.
  Includes bibliographical references (p.).
  ISBN-13: 978-1-58980-248-3 (hardcover : alk. paper)
  1. Interpersonal relations—Religious aspects—Christianity. 2. Pastoral
theology. I. Bozeman, Jeanine Cannon. II. Smith, Argile Asa, 1955-

  BV4597.52.I57 2004
  248.8'92—dc22

                              2004014006

The *King James Version* of the Bible has been used for references
throughout this book unless otherwise indicated.

Printed in the United States of America
Published by Pelican Publishing Company, Inc.
1000 Burmaster Street, Gretna, Louisiana 70053

This book is dedicated
in memory of
Jeanine Cannon Bozeman's father
Henry Oliver Cannon
who modeled nurturing interpersonal relationships.
This book is also dedicated to
Dr. Lorena Smith
and
in memory of
Dr. Dumas Smith
Argile Smith's aunt and uncle
for their lifelong devotion to Great Commandment relationships.

Contents

Preface

The idea for this book came to our minds as we designed a seminary course to help our students to develop healthy interpersonal relationship skills. We knew that a seminary curriculum needed to include such a course, and we had the support of our administration to design it. But we couldn't find a suitable book for what we wanted to do in the course.

We decided that the best way to secure a book that would meet our needs was to develop it ourselves. The book we had in mind would not only contain information on some basic interpersonal communication skills, it would also provide insights about nurturing healthy relationships in ministry. Inviting the expertise of ministers who are doing Kingdom work in a variety of settings to join us in the project, we set out to produce just such a book.

If you are a seminary student interested in nurturing healthy interpersonal relationships, the articles in this book will help you. They cover a wide range of issues that you will face in ministry, issues that move beyond the arena of technique and get at the heart and soul of effective ministry.

But this book will be helpful for other ministers as well. If you are a minister at work in the Kingdom task to which God has called you, this book can affirm the ways in which you have made progress in interpersonal relationships. And it can suggest some areas that still need your attention and some ways for you to address them.

If you are a denominational leader, the book will helpful to you too. It could be the resource you have been looking for, a book that you can pass along to ministers who come to you for advice in the area of healthy relationships with people who share with them in Kingdom work.

If you are a church member, you may find this book to be helpful too. It can help you come to an understanding of the complex set of relationships a minister needs to strengthen in order to be effective in ministry. Accordingly, it can show you some specific ways that you can pray for and support the ministers in your church.

We have developed the book in the hope that it will help ministers to nurture healthy interpersonal relationships. For us, relationships in ministry matter more than techniques. Techniques come and go, but relationships last. In fact, they last forever.

The Editors

Acknowledgments

We have many people to thank for this book. Without their help, it would have never gotten this far.

The faculty and administration of New Orleans Baptist Theological Seminary affirmed us as we worked on the project. Also, they challenged us to think clearly about the task at hand to make sure that we kept ministers in mind.

The students who have enrolled in our course on interpersonal relationship skills showed us when we were making progress with the ideas expressed in the book. And they also let us know when an idea wasn't worth pursuing.

The ministers at work in the settings to which God had called them studied our material from their perspectives. Their suggestions and rebuttals helped us to rethink some of our ideas and to express them better.

Other people in the churches read our material too. They made valuable comments that prompted us to include their voices in the discussion of the ideas in the book.

Pam Cole turned more than two dozen articles on interpersonal relationship skills into a workable manuscript. Bill McCall worked on the manuscript too.

Pelican Publishing Company agreed to publish our book. They have helped us to extend our ideas past the seminary classroom into the churches and other settings in which ministers are trying to strengthen their interpersonal relationship skills so they can be effective in their ministries.

The Lord gave us what we couldn't give ourselves as we worked on the book. We are grateful to Him most of all.

The Contributors

The people who wrote the articles for this book serve the Lord in a variety of ministry settings. Two of them are ministry couples whose service in churches has given them helpful insights about a minister's family. Three writers are ministry specialists who have devoted themselves to working side by side with churches and the ministers who serve them. Thirteen writers are associated with theological education that is dedicated to helping ministers to do Kingdom work well. The articles they have written reflect their devotion to the Lord, experience in ministry, commitment to excellence, and interest in helping ministers. Getting to know them will give you an even greater appreciation for their contributions to this book.

Ministry Couples

Fred and Elizabeth Luter wrote the testimony titled "Relationships at Church." A dynamic preacher and leader, Fred is the pastor of Franklin Avenue Baptist Church in New Orleans, Louisiana. His wife, Elizabeth, is a distinguished Bible teacher in and beyond the church. They provide an excellent example of marriage and family life for ministers.

Argile and Connie Smith wrote "Sharing the Joys and Sorrows in Ministry." Before Argile joined the faculty at New Orleans Baptist Theological Seminary (NOBTS), he was a pastor. For fifteen years of pastoral ministry, he and Connie worked together to strike a balance between church work and home life.

Ministry Specialists

Jane Bishop, M.A.C.E., M.R.E., wrote "Singleness and Ministry." Jane serves as a team leader for Missionary Mobilization at the North American Mission Board of the Southern Baptist Convention. Her work involves the rewarding but challenging task of placing missionaries where they are most needed in North America.

Wallace T. Davis, Ph.D., wrote "The Importance of Community Ministry and Interpersonal Relationships." Dr. Davis is president and chief executive officer of Volunteers of America Southeast in Mobile, Alabama. Before he began his ministry with VOA, he was a pastor who led his congregation to be intentional about ministering in the community.

Joe N. McKeever, D.Min., wrote "Learning to Listen." Dr. McKeever is the Director of Missions for the Baptist Association of Greater New Orleans. Previously he served as pastor of the First Baptist Church of Kenner, Louisiana. A seasoned pastor, he is also a gifted writer and cartoonist. His work has been published in a variety of books, journals, and newspapers.

Seminary Faculty

Jerry N. Barlow, Th.D., wrote "Relating to the Church Staff." Dr. Barlow is Dean of Graduate Studies and Professor of Preaching and Pastoral Work at NOBTS. Prior to joining the faculty, he served as pastor of the First Baptist Church of Franklinton, Louisiana. He continues to serve in the churches as an interim pastor and a consultant.

Jeanine Cannon Bozeman, Ph.D., wrote four articles for the book: "Nurturing a Healthy Self-Concept," "Developing Communication Skills," "Learning to Relate to Difficult People," and "Decision Making." She is Professor of Social Work at NOBTS, where she also served as Chair of the Division of Christian Education Ministries.

Kristyn Carver, M.A.M.F.C., co-wrote "Examining Messages from Our Families." Kristyn is Instructor of Psychology and Counseling at Leavell College of NOBTS. A doctoral candidate as well as a teacher, she is writing her dissertation, titled "An

Analysis of the Gender Differences in the Cognitive, Affective, and Behavioral Domains of Forgiveness."

Cara Cochran, M.Div., M.A.M.F.C., co-wrote "Rewriting Your Family Story." Cara is Instructor and Assistant to the Academic Dean at Psychological Studies Institute (PSI). She is also a doctoral candidate. Her dissertation is titled "Theological Integration in Counselor Education: An Analysis of Knowledge and Application of Students of the Psychological Studies Institute."

Philip A. Coyle, Ph.D., co-wrote "Rewriting Your Family Story." Dr. Coyle is Academic Dean and Professor of Psychology and Counseling at Psychological Studies Institute (PSI) in Chattanooga, Tennessee. Prior to assuming his present position at PSI, he was Professor of Psychology and Counseling at NOBTS. He has done extensive research in the area of family systems.

Steve Echols, Ph.D., D.Min., wrote two articles about relationships in the context of the church: "Emotional Intelligence and Spiritual Maturity" and "Building a Culture for Managing Church Conflict." Dr. Echols is Associate Dean of Professional Doctoral Programs and Associate Professor of Leadership at NOBTS. In addition, he is the pastor of a local church.

Rhonda H. Kelley, Ph.D., wrote "Dining Etiquette." Dr. Kelley is Professor of Women's Ministry at Leavell College of NOBTS, where she also directs the Women's Ministry programs and the Student Wives Certificate of Excellence program. She has distinguished herself as a gifted lecturer and writer. Her husband, Dr. Chuck Kelley, is President of NOBTS.

Carol Lemke wrote the testimony titled "Being a Minister's Wife." Dr. Steve Lemke, her husband, is Provost at NOBTS. Carol is a guest lecturer in seminary classes, and her testimony about being a minister's wife offers valuable insights for ministers who want to nurture strong relationships in their homes.

W. Dan Parker, D.Min., wrote the testimony titled "A Church Touching the Community." Dr. Parker is Director of the Undergraduate Extension Center System and Associate

Professor of Pastoral Ministries at NOBTS. While serving as a seminary professor and administrator, he is also a pastor. His testimony shows how a church can make a lasting impact on the community.

Loretta G. Rivers, M.S.W., wrote "How to Work with Other Helping Professionals." Loretta is Instructor of Social Work at NOBTS. A doctoral candidate, she is writing her dissertation on grief and bereavement services in nursing homes. Along with her academic work, she expresses her love for senior adults by spending time each week at a local nursing home as a Bible teacher.

Argile Smith, Ph.D., wrote two articles: "Forgiving" and "Receiving the Blessing." Dr. Smith also wrote the testimony titled "Getting Dad's Approval." He is Professor of Preaching, occupying the J. D. Grey Chair of Preaching, and also serves as Chair of the Division of Pastoral Ministries at NOBTS. In addition, he serves in churches as an interim pastor.

Asa R. Sphar III, Ph.D., co-wrote "Examining Messages from Our Families." Dr. Sphar is Professor of Psychology and Counseling at NOBTS and is also Director of Clinical Training. Devoted to integrating theology and psychology, he developed a reconciliation-focused counseling theory aimed at helping hurting people strengthen their relationships with God, others, and themselves.

Margaret F. Williamson, Ph.D., wrote "Being Assertive." Dr. Williamson is Assistant Professor of Christian Education and Associate Director of the Extension Center System at NOBTS. She brings her experience in local church ministry to her work as a professor and administrator. Her articles and Bible studies have been published in a variety of denominational periodicals.

Introduction

In seminaries across the country, professors work with students on developing the basic skills for effective ministry. Under the careful watch of their professors, students preparing for a life of ministry learn how to interpret the Bible, how to discern and articulate doctrine, how to prepare and deliver sermons or Bible studies, how to evangelize, how to counsel, how to lead, how to handle administrative issues, how to design and direct worship services, and how to perform weddings, funerals, and even parent-baby dedications.

Eventually the students graduate, get into the churches, and put the skills they have learned to good use. Some skills are used more than others, depending on the ministry setting, with one exception. No matter what the ministry setting may be, a minister's interpersonal relationship skills will always be put to work. Ministers can count on those skills in particular to be stretched frequently as they serve the Lord in the Kingdom assignment He has given them. For that reason, a minister's interpersonal relationship skills need to be strengthened just like any other set of skills for effective ministry.

Strengthening interpersonal relationship skills, however, involves more than simply learning a few techniques. In order to improve the skills, ministers do well to explore the nature of relationships themselves, how they function together, and where they begin. For trustworthy insights to guide us in such an exploration, we turn to Scripture.

One of the best-known passages in God's Word, the Great Commandment, provides the foundation for healthy interpersonal relationships in ministry. In this commandment, the Lord directs us to appreciate the value of our relationships with other people and even ourselves. At the heart of the commandment, however, is the mandate to love God.[1] Our deepening and maturing love for Him prompts us to establish and maintain loving relationships in the same way. Specifically, your relationship with the Lord affects five important relationships in your life and ministry.

First, your relationship with the Lord has a distinct bearing on your relationship with yourself. As you grow in your love for the Lord, you are able to see yourself as He sees you. Seeing yourself through His eyes strengthens your self-concept. Also, it helps you to live in gratitude for the blessing He has given you in His Son. You can live thankfully in the humbling reality that He has saved you and called you to be a minister.

Second, your relationship with the Lord shapes your relationships with the people in your family. The family setting in which you grew up may have been a good environment, one that helped you to proceed from childhood to adolescence and on to adulthood. Or it could have been a bad environment filled with pain and struggle. As you grow in your relationship with the Lord, you can trust Him to help you account for the bad as well as the good in ways that will bring honor to Him in your ministry.

Third, your relationship with the Lord influences your marriage and parenting relationships. Loving Him can deepen your love for the person who married you and the children God has given you. Also, it can inspire you to make your marriage and your children a high priority in your ministry. If you are single, your relationship with Him can instill within you the definite awareness that wholeness results from knowing Jesus Christ personally, not from having a husband or a wife.

Fourth, your relationship with the Lord guides you as you give attention to the relationships in your church. Most of the people in your congregation get along with each other well. But a few of them can be difficult. Likewise, church staff and other church leaders usually work well together. But periodically conflicts can arise and set them at odds with each other. Loving the Lord can help you learn to love His people all the time, when situations look sublime and when they look stressful.

Fifth, your relationship with the Lord nurtures your love for your community. Fear of the community in which you serve can allow you to cloister yourself and your congregation away from the people God has called you to reach. But love casts out fear.[2] God's love in you can motivate you to be moved with compassion and to reach out to people in the community with the gospel of Christ. It can also inspire you to work with other helping professionals in the community.

You probably agree with the confident assertion that the Great Commandment is the bedrock for an exploration into interpersonal relationships for effective ministry. And you also likely appreciate the affirmation that our relationship with the Lord affects our interpersonal relationships. Consequently, you will undoubtedly understand that any inquiry into interpersonal relationship skills for ministry has to begin with an investigation into your relationship with God.

As you investigate your walk with God, consider some basic questions to ask yourself. The following questions should help you get off to a good start in your personal inventory: Have you received Christ as your Savior and Lord? Have you surrendered to His call to ministry? Have you given attention to the spiritual disciplines related to reading and meditating on His Word as well as praying? Are you willing to obey Him? Are you nurturing the mind of Christ? Do you want nothing more than to be the kind of minister that would please Him?

Effective ministry involves healthy relationships as much as reliable techniques. And healthy relationships begin with the Lord. You can trust Him to help you develop the interpersonal relationship skills necessary for effective ministry.

INTERPERSONAL RELATIONSHIP SKILLS FOR MINISTERS

PART I

Your Relationship with Yourself

CHAPTER 1

Nurturing a Healthy Self-Concept

Jeanine Cannon Bozeman

Most of us want to be successful in interpersonal relationships. Reports from churches, however, indicate poor interpersonal relationships as the primary reason that some ministers are being fired from their positions. Such reports compel us to examine ourselves and evaluate our interpersonal relationship skills.

Two major factors determine the success of our interpersonal relationships: our self-concept and our skill in communication. In our consideration of our self-concept, we will explore a variety of insights that will help us appreciate the value of this critical interpersonal relationship factor.

Biblical Basis

Our worth is bestowed on us by God. The Bible places great worth and value upon the individual. The fact that we were created in the image of God indicates our importance in His eyes.[1] Because the Bible reveals that God esteems His highest creation, we should be able to esteem ourselves too.

The Mosaic law declares, "Thou shalt love thy neighbour as thyself" (Lev. 19:18). This law teaches that a healthy concern for one's self and one's own well-being is natural and God-implanted. Esteeming one's self is assumed to be a normal human attitude that is to give rise to esteem for others. The same kind of care and concern for oneself is to be extended to others.[2]

The writer of Psalm 8 emphasized the importance and glory

of humanity. Clifton Allen stated that God was so concerned with man that He made him only a "little bit diminished from God and circled him round with honor and pride."[3] The psalmist revealed that man was created by God for a high purpose: to serve as God's deputy in the world, a God-appointed king over creation.[4] The royal position of a human being was manifested in the fact that he was expected to have dominion over creation.[5] Again, we have been regarded as beings of worth and should thus value ourselves.[6]

Psalms 22 and 35 also provide interesting words that suggest our value as human beings. The writer of these psalms referred to himself as "my darling."[7] Thomas Welby Bozeman was a student of Harold L. Rutledge, a psychology and counseling professor at New Orleans Baptist Theological Seminary. He indicated that Rutledge translated "my darling" to mean "my precious self" or "my worthy self."[8] In other words, the psalmist looked upon himself as a worthy being.

Jesus summarized the commandments when He declared that we are to love our neighbor as ourselves.[9] In emphasizing the importance of loving God and neighbor, Jesus also emphasized that we are to love ourselves. A godly love must include a love for self.[10] As Allen said, "Either one loves God, neighbor and himself or he loves neither."[11] Love cannot be divided; for self cannot be separated from God or neighbor.[12] Jesus affirmed, "Are not two sparrows sold for a farthing? and one of them shall not fall on the ground without your Father. But the very hairs of your head are numbered. Fear ye not therefore, ye are of more value than many sparrows" (Matt. 10:29-31). In this passage, Jesus stressed the infinite value of people. The God who cares for the smallest things also cares for persons, who are so much more important.[13]

Paul Ramsey commented on the command "Love thy neighbour as thyself" and revealed how we are to love ourselves. He wrote, "Self love does not wait on worth. In fact it is the other way around: self love makes you desire worth for yourself."[14]

Christians who believe the Bible and accept the fact that God loves them unconditionally should be able to accept their worth as persons. The worth of the person was assumed in the gospel of Jesus Christ. God has created us; Jesus has redeemed us. Because the grace of God has emancipated us from low self-esteem, we should be able to mature in confidence to the place in which we can value ourselves.[15]

Psychological Foundation

In addition to a biblical basis for self-esteem, a number of noteworthy psychologists have recognized our need for a healthy self-esteem. They have observed a distinct relationship between the level of a person's self-esteem and his or her mental health. They also have noted the relationship between self-esteem and behavior in such vital areas of life as work, love, and human relationships.[16]

One of these early psychologists was Alfred Adler, a Viennese psychiatrist who lived from 1870 to 1937. He originated the concept of the "inferiority complex." Adler contended that feelings of inferiority grow out of the child's inferior position in life. The child is aware that he or she cannot handle the demands of daily existence alone. The feelings of inferiority may be intensified further by parents who have the habit of not taking the child seriously, thus leaving the child with the impression that he or she is a nobody. The child may retain this impression into adulthood.[17] Likewise, physical disabilities and differences in physical size and strength also may contribute to feelings of inferiority. Adler saw the need to overcome feelings of inferiority as a very important issue for individuals who struggle with self-esteem problems.[18]

Psychologist Karen Horney developed the theory of the idealized image, which plays a major role in self-evaluation. According to her theory, a person forms an idealized self because he or she despises his or her real self and, therefore, fluctuates between self-love and self-contempt.[19] Horney isolated three basic needs among people: (1) the need to move toward people, such as the need for love; (2) the need to move away from people, or the need for independence; and (3) the need to move against people, or the need for power.[20] The way an individual reacts to these three needs will reveal the level of his or her self-esteem.[21]

Gordon Allport was a psychologist who recognized the role of self-esteem in social interactions. He theorized that self-esteem is closely tied to the need for autonomy. If the need for autonomy is thwarted in childhood, for example, the child will suffer a blow to his or her self-esteem. According to Allport, all of a person's actions aim at the goal of keeping one's self-esteem as healthy as possible.[22]

Erick Fromm, a psychoanalyst, focused on the loneliness of individuals and pointed out that we are lonely because we do not love or trust ourselves. He believed that persons have to love themselves before they could love others.[23] He also taught that selfishness is the opposite of real love and insisted that we must learn to love ourselves in a healthy way in order to overcome selfishness.[24]

Client-centered therapist Carl Rogers emphasized that unconditional positive regard enables a person to know and accept himself or herself. This unconditional positive regard enables people to reevaluate and accept themselves as individuals worthy of respect.[25]

Abraham Maslow stressed the need that all persons have for a high evaluation of themselves for a healthy self-esteem. He also related self-esteem to issues of security and insecurity. For instance, an individual who is high in self-esteem and is also secure will be able to be kind, cooperative, and friendly. However, persons who are high in self-esteem but are insecure may seek to dominate and hurt others. They may even become hostile and aggressive.[26]

Sidney Jourard, a professor of psychology, accented our need to disclose ourselves to at least one significant person. Jourard taught that the knowledge of self is necessary for one to be able to love oneself and others in a healthy manner.[27]

Basic Components

Self-concept includes certain components that a person has differentiated as definite and fairly stable characteristics of oneself.[28] Three components comprise the self-concept: self-confidence, self-esteem, and self-sufficiency. Self-confidence is the belief in ourselves and our ability. Self-esteem is the evaluation we place upon ourselves or a personal judgment of worthiness. Self-sufficiency is the dependence we place upon the viewpoint of others. In reality, most people are not thinking of us because they are focused upon their own lives, problems, and desires. Self-sufficiency has to do with how we think and feel others think and feel about us.[29] If we are low in self-sufficiency, it means we need a great deal of affirmation from people who have significance in our life.

As we evaluate ourselves, we do well to remember that with the help of God, we can develop more positive self-concepts. Also, we can ask Him to help us to be aware of influences that affect us throughout our lives and definitely influence our view of ourselves.

Some Influences

Our self-concept is shaped through interactions, primarily with parents, but also with other important people in our lives. Specifically, self-esteem is learned from the foundational interactions in childhood. Other influences that shape our self-esteem occur during adolescence and adulthood.[30]

The childhood stage generally involves the first twelve years. During this stage many factors help to shape a child's self-esteem. For example, a parent's reaction to a child's need to go to the bathroom or explore his or her own body will influence the child's self-esteem. Other influences may be the child's ordinal position and the economic standing of the family. Coopersmith found that four areas of influence seem to have the greatest influence upon a child's self-esteem: acceptance, discipline, democratic practices, and independence.[31]

Parental acceptance helps to build a child's self-esteem. Warm and accepting parents convey to the child that he or she is worthy. Parents may express their acceptance of a child through devotion to the child's interests, health, activities, and needs as well as an unconditional love and approval which help a child to develop basic trust.[32] We generally think that all parents immediately accept their babies. In actuality, parents reflect their disappointment at the birth of their child because they wanted a boy and got a girl or because the baby was not as "perfect" as they anticipated. Often the parents' response results in their child's low view of self, which is observed often in the child's lack of love and spontaneity in his or her relationships.

Also, discipline appears to influence a child's level of self-esteem. Discipline needs to be firm and loving with clearly established limits. Coopersmith's conclusion was that the greater the structure, the greater the self-esteem. Higher expectations by parents give the child a feeling of importance. Consistency in discipline was another factor that appeared to be essential for healthy self-esteem.[33]

Likewise, parents influence their children in building healthy self-esteem by using democratic procedures in the home. Rules are established and limitations set, but parents permit the opinions of the children and their expression of feelings. The democratic atmosphere will assist the child in considering himself or herself a person of worth.[34]

Moreover, the development of independence in a child appears to affect feelings of self-worth. Parents who give their child an opportunity to trust himself or herself enable the child to develop independence and also grow in his or her feelings of self-worth.

When children feel accepted by their parents, perceive that rules are defined clearly and enforced consistently, are given freedom to express their opinions and feelings, and are encouraged to establish a sense of independence, they will grow up feeling that they are individuals of worth. Persons must experience love and care in their earliest years in order to become tender, loving human beings.[35]

Adolescents appear to be deeply concerned with their self-image. During the adolescent years, three areas of influence help shape self-esteem: relationships, achievements, and self-evaluation.

Relationships with significant people influence the adolescent's self-esteem. These significant people may include parents, teachers, counselors, pastors, youth pastors, coaches, and peer groups. Relationships can convey to the teenager that he or she is, important and a person of worth and value. For instance, I remember a high-school algebra teacher who accepted me as a worthwhile person. She affirmed my ability and helped me to see that there was a wider world than the village in which I grew up.

The achievement level of the adolescent influences the level of his or her self-esteem.[36] These achievements may include scholastic honors, sports involvement, and extracurricular activities such as band or music.

Another area of influence upon the adolescent's self-esteem is personal evaluation. An adolescent may need help in order to evaluate his or her body, abilities, and potential as a person.

The influences of adulthood give shape to our personalities. None of us have "arrived" yet. We are constantly in the process of maturing. Four areas of influence upon the adult's self-esteem seem to be important: relationships, autonomy, success, and control.[37]

Relationships continue to be a vital influence upon the adult's self-esteem. When adults experience satisfying relationships, they are able to value and respect themselves.

Autonomy is an important factor in an adult's self-esteem. When individuals discover for themselves what is right and true, they can then govern their actions by what they think or determine is right and true. Such individuals do not depend on another person's values, opinions, and judgments.

Success or achievements influence self-esteem for an adult. Success as defined by a person's desires and ambitions is a significant factor.

The ability of an adult to control or discipline himself or herself will influence self-esteem. An adult must be able to make appropriate emotional responses in order to maintain self-esteem. Lack of ability to control emotions may result in loss of self-esteem.

Some Problems

Self-esteem is a vital issue in family problems. Low self-esteem can cause personal problems, husband-wife problems, and parent-child problems.[38]

Personal adjustment dependent on one's self-esteem includes emotional life, ability to learn, and creativeness. Self-esteem also influences social adjustment. Persons who are low in their feelings of self-worth are likely to withdraw from personal relationships.[39]

Lack of self-esteem may result also in husband-wife problems. Some of these problems are jealousy, criticism, and sexual difficulties. Jealousy is caused frequently by feelings of inadequacy. A person who feels insecure is more likely to be critical of others. Persons low in self-esteem tend to build themselves up by tearing down others. Also, the lack of self-esteem can cause difficulty in sexual adjustment. The level of an individual's self-esteem appears to affect the individual's ability to give and receive love.

Lack of appropriate self-esteem may result in difficulties in parent-child relationships. A couple will be good parents only as they build a strong relationship with each other. The strength of the relationship between a husband and wife will affect their ability to provide unconditional acceptance, appropriate discipline, democratic practices, and opportunities for independence that will build self-esteem in each child.[40]

Persons low in self-esteem can improve their view of themselves by living consciously, accepting themselves, accepting responsibility, being assertive, living purposefully, and developing integrity.[41] In addition, persons may examine their past lives and reframe negative messages, be aware of their own significance to God and others, develop a keen awareness of past successes, evaluate their moral expectations, and live responsibly.[42]

We do not have to be victims of our past or environment. We can develop a healthy sense of self-esteem through the recognition of the worth bestowed upon us by God. Also, we can seek His guidance as we nurture a healthy self-concept in ourselves and our children.

CHAPTER 2

Developing Communication Skills
Jeanine Cannon Bozeman

As human beings we have a basic need for interpersonal relationships. God created us with relationships in mind. According to Genesis 2:18, it was not good for man to be alone. All of us long to be understood and to understand others with whom we choose to relate. In order to connect to others we need to develop the skill of communication.

In this article, communication will be explored in the context of marriage relationships. Principles of communication will be applied in that context.

Communication is essential in intimate relationships. The key to the whole process of building intimacy in the marital relationship is skill in communication. The quality of communication determines how a marriage relationship is established and how it changes over time.[1] Communication was recognized by David and Vera Mace as the "master key" in the marriage relationship: "As we have sometimes expressed it, relationships-in-depth can only be achieved and can only be sustained through communication-in-depth."[2]

Virginia Satir is a therapist who also has been called a communication specialist.[3] She expressed her conviction about the importance of communication in the marital relationship by noting that boredom is a leading cause of divorce, stating, "If a husband and wife begin to have sterile and lifeless encounters, they eventually become bored with one another."[4]

Since communication is emphasized by therapists, counselors, and family life specialists, ministers should give it consideration too. How do we define communication? Communication is not a monologue in which one talks to oneself. Real communication is a dialogue, a meeting of meanings, "a reciprocal relationship in which each party experiences the other side."[5] Communication involves a sender, a receiver, and a message; so problems may occur with any of these three components. Authentic communication takes place when the receiver hears the message that was intended by the sender. As Satir has said in a number of conferences, communication takes place when "you receive in your glass what I have poured from my pitcher." Accordingly, communication is best understood as a meeting of meanings.

Communication Problems

Various communication problems may develop in the marital relationship as well as in any other relationship. These problems involve systems, barriers, verbal communication, and nonverbal communication.

Within the marriage partnership, one of the problems in communication concerns the systems involved in the union. A marriage involves three different but interdependent systems: the system of the total being of the male; the system of the total being of the female; and the marital system, deriving from the interaction of the male and female systems joined together.[6] The term *system* indicates that each position is related to the other, and a change in one system results in changes in the other systems.[7] There are two kinds of marital systems—closed and open. The main difference between them is the specific reaction to change from the outside. An open system provides for change; a closed one provides for little or no change.[8]

Systems have rules that help to maintain a sense of equilibrium. Rules are a vital, dynamic, and influential force in family life. Rules may be explicit or implicit, rigid or flexible, and are brought from the family of origin to the new marital system. Consequently, a couple may be living according to some communication rules from their families of origin that may be affecting their present relationships. Rules determine what can be talked about, how it can be talked about, and to whom it can be talked about.

Another possible problem in communication has to do with barriers. A barrier to communication is something that keeps meanings from meeting. Possible barriers to effective communication are images, anxieties, defensiveness, contrary purposes, withholding, lack of clarity, and coded messages.

Images which participants in communication have of one another can be barriers to communication. Likewise, images which participants in communication have of the subject matter can obstruct communication.

The anxieties of partners to communication are a second barrier that hampers partners from speaking and responding to one another with meaning. These anxieties may be either personal anxieties or anxieties about the subject matter. Anxieties become evident in defensive remarks and distortions of meaning that partners use in the fear of being understood as well as in the fear of being misunderstood.[9]

A third barrier to marital communication is defensiveness. Each of us functions with well-established defenses in the interest of our personal well-being. Some of our common defenses are justification, projection, or blaming others for something for which we are responsible. Defensiveness of any kind is a barrier to effective marital communication.[10]

A fourth barrier to the meeting of meanings is contrary purposes. In a marriage, one spouse may be interested only in securing agreement with his or her point of view. As a result, he or she may not really hear what the other says.

A fifth barrier to effective marital communication is withholding information from one's spouse. A common form of withholding in marital communication is the lack of disclosure or openness. Self-disclosure involves the dropping of pretenses and the revealing of the real self to the partner. Withholding between intimates is destructive, but disclosure is constructive. The importance of sharing ideas, thoughts, and feelings must be nurtured throughout the marriage relationship.[11]

Lack of clarity is a sixth major communication barrier and a cause of breakdown in otherwise workable marriages. The communication between husband and wife demands the clearest message sending possible if the relationship is to grow instead of die. Accurate or clear communication is communication that reduces uncertainty.

A seventh barrier to meaning in the marriage union involves the sending of coded messages. A coded message is a communication, verbal or nonverbal, which must be decoded before it can be understood properly. Cecil Osborne described the coded message as a plea for someone to meet one's needs without those needs being expressed clearly. He added that "this is as unrealistic as expecting someone to understand Arabic without having studied it. Communication demands an honest expression of one's feelings and needs."[12]

Two kinds of communication occur between husband and wife: verbal and nonverbal. Both kinds can be accompanied by a variety of problems.

Some communication problems involve errors in sending verbal messages. These errors may be manifested in various ways such as timing, incongruence, and double-bind messages.

Timing is considered an important principle in effective communication. L. Richard Lessor stressed the importance of timing: "There are times during the day and night when a person is at his strongest, at his most open, at his weakest, at his most closed."[13] Partners often give each other "leftover" time. The quality of leftover time is never sufficient to nourish a marriage. I have learned in my marriage relationship that timing is crucial in our communication. In the morning when my husband is reading the paper is not a good time to send a message.

Incongruence is another possible problem in sending messages. Incongruent communication is one in which two or more messages, sent at different levels, contradict each other. In these messages, something does not fit. These double-level messages may be considered to be unhealthy when they are not commented upon or acknowledged in some way by the one to whom they are directed.[14]

Contradictory messages are often referred to as double-bind messages. These messages play a central role in dysfunctional marital communication. The victim is doomed to rejection no matter how he or she responds.

Errors in communication between husband and wife can occur in receiving messages. Two major issues associated with receiving messages are listening and feedback.

In marriage counseling I frequently hear the complaint "My husband (or wife) doesn't listen to me." Deep listening is seeing the world through another's eyes. One of the greatest needs among intimates is to have the experience of deep sharing. Deep listening is essential for the partners. John W. Drakeford maintained that the "lack of listening is probably the greatest point of failure in most marriages."[15]

Paul Tournier assessed that it is impossible to overemphasize the immense need persons have to be really listened to, to be understood. He asserted, "No one can develop freely in this world and find a full life without feeling understood by at least one person."[16]

Feedback is another problem issue in receiving messages. Feedback is a response on the part of the recipient of the message that indicates that the message has been received and understood. In giving feedback the receiver tries to re-express his or her understanding of what the sender said. A mate can give the partner feedback by paraphrasing the statement received to make sure he or she understood it, by asking questions, or by making a responsive statement that tells how he or she feels about the matter.

Approximately 70 percent of the communication between husbands and wives is nonverbal.[17] The way in which one walks, drums fingers, smiles, frowns, and touches are important forms of nonverbal communication. Ambiguous, nonverbal communication can have many possible meanings, and interpretations are not always correct. Therefore, nonverbal messages should be thought of as clues, not facts.

Communication Patterns

Communication problems appear to be numerous in the marital relationship, but they can be reduced significantly by understanding and analyzing the patterns of communication and the ego states from which the couple habitually speak. Once they come to an understanding of the problem, they can begin to make appropriate changes.

Satir and Shostrom have proposed that people develop patterns of communication that they use under stress. Four of these patterns of communication are counterproductive because they are incongruent and manipulative. They are placating, blaming, being super-reasonable or like a computer, and being irrelevant.[18]

In the placating pattern, the person desires peace at any price. The placater thinks of himself or herself as worth nothing and being responsible for everything that goes wrong.[19] As a placater, the message could be, "I'm a worm, and I stay here because you allow it." I, personally, find a placater to be a weak, nonassertive, and passive person.

Blaming is an alternative communication pattern that people sometimes choose in order to protect themselves. The blamer is a faultfinder, a dictator, and a boss. He or she acts superior and cuts down everything and everyone. Such persons are more interested in throwing their weight around than in communicating with other persons.

An additional way to communicate under stress is to be super-reasonable, or like a computer. The computer is very reasonable, but it shows no feeling. A person who displays this characteristic is interested in facts, not feelings. Most women, because they are wired for relationships, have difficulty relating to such people because they seem so cold and unemotional.

A fourth choice of incongruent communication is to be irrelevant. This person can be labeled as a distracter. The distracter's words are unrelated to anything that is going on in the interaction. You probably have had the experience of attempting to communicate with a distracter and felt totally frustrated in the process.

All four of these patterns of communication are incongruent, and all become means of avoiding intimacy. They result in estrangement and isolation because persons are not connected to each other.[20]

A fifth pattern of communication is the leveling pattern. In this pattern all parts of the message match—the voice tone, the facial expression, and the body language. This response is real and genuine. Levelers show their feelings and can say what they want. A leveling response has the possibility of healing ruptures, resolving disagreements, and building bridges between people. Being a leveler enables a person to have honesty, intimacy, and creativity. As leveling is practiced, distances between people are reduced. Leveling is the goal of intimate communication.[21]

Improving Communication

In examining our communication, it is helpful to determine which of the ego states is being expressed. In the parent ego state, a speaker assumes an authoritarian and superior tone and talks down to the receiver. The speaker conveys the message "I have a right to tell you what to do." Frequently used words from this ego state are "ought" and "should." Speaking from this ego state and using this tone usually creates rebellion and opposition from the receiver.

A second ego state we use is the child ego state. From this state we express our emotions, usually selfish and self-centered, such as our personal feelings and our sexual desires.

A third ego state that we use in transactions with others is the adult ego state. From this ego state factual messages are sent, and information is processed.

Each ego state is appropriate at different times and in different situations. We will find it helpful to be aware of which state we use most frequently and with whom. Feedback from others will help us evaluate our communication. After evaluation, we may decide we need to improve our communication.

Some general principles may be helpful to us personally and in guiding other individuals and couples to improve communication in intimate relationships. Among these principles are:

1. Acknowledge the importance of communication. Be aware that it is the greatest single factor affecting any relationship.

2. Diagnose and discuss the effectiveness of your present level of communication. Own up to yourself that you may block communication through various maneuvers.
3. Make yourself open and crystal clear. Be available.
4. Share your private view of your world with your partner.
5. Choose the time to discuss your situation.
6. Focus on your own communication, not your partner's.
7. Decide on equal time.
8. Don't be discouraged if at first the discussion is not successful.
9. Express your feelings.
10. Learn to listen to the complete message.
11. Check out messages.
12. Share things you appreciate about each other.
13. Learn to express conflict.
14. Be specific when you introduce a gripe or complaint.
15. Avoid sarcasm.
16. Talk as adult to adult and do not assume the role of parent, teacher, or therapist.
17. Avoid making assumptions.
18. Be willing to take more than half of the responsibility for the effectiveness of the communication whether as sender or receiver.
19. Talk about your needs.
20. Express your fears.

Because effective communication is so important in marriage and family relationships, seeking to improve personal communication is a worthy goal. Improvement in the area of communication will result in more nurturing, intimate relationships.

CHAPTER 3

Learning to Listen

Joe N. McKeever

In a heated conversation with a church member one day, she said, "You're not listening to me!" I answered, "I am listening; I just disagree with you." Later, when I recounted that conversation to my wife, she said, "Whenever someone accuses you of not listening, they mean they do not feel you are making an effort to understand what they are saying."

Dennis the Menace, banished to the corner by bad behavior, called back to his mother, "I hear you, but I'm not listening!" Therein lies the problem.

Because listening is such a complex activity that takes place on so many different levels, it's a wonder any of us understand what the other is saying. Through the years I have accumulated at least a half-dozen books just on the subject of being quiet and listening. As one who from childhood would rather talk than listen, I can now see that the Father has been working with me on this problem all my life. Sometimes the timing of His lessons is so right it's almost scary. Take the other day, for instance.

After my wife's observation that the person who said I wasn't listening felt I wasn't trying to understand, I ran by a fast food place for a few minutes. As I sat down at the table, I noticed the drinking cup was filthy. A coating of rust lined the lip of the cup. No doubt the manager would want to know about it, I reasoned, so I walked to the counter and told her about the cup.

"Sir, that was the last cup in the dispenser," she explained. "It picked up that rusty residue from butting up against the end."

"Well, perhaps you ought to clean the inside of the dispenser," I said.

"We do," she said, "but the last cup always comes out looking like that."

I stood there, realizing the manager was responding to my words, but not to my concern. She heard my speech, but not my heart. I did not need an explanation. I wanted her to appreciate how a customer feels on finding his drinking cup dirty and to assure me she would take steps to see that it never happened again.

It is not enough to hear words. We must listen to what people mean. Our Lord must have had this thought in mind when He said, "He who has ears to hear, let him hear." To the disciples He said, "Blessed are . . . your ears, for they hear" (Matt. 13:9, 16).

Someone has pointed out that the English language is composed of 600,000 words, of which we use about 2,000 on a regular basis. Of those, 500 have some 14,000 definitions. Some words actually carry more than 100 different meanings.[1] That any of us can make sense of the other is nothing less than a miracle!

The Failure to Listen

Many good people practice a sin of omission when they fail to listen. My wife and I have a family member who seems unable to hear a word we say. Our phone calls become endless monologues on her part that leave us drained and exhausted.

At a television station, I stood off camera and watched a friend conduct her talk show. In one of the short segments, she interviewed a preacher who had come to town to speak in a local church the next day. The exchange went like this:

Interviewer: "Reverend Lancaster, welcome to the city!"

Minister: "Thank you so much. You know, as I travel around this world, I see people of all types in all kinds of situations. I was in India last month, and next week I'll be in Canada. I see lots of people. But there's one thing I've noticed: they all have the same spiritual needs. And I like to tell them that the remedy for their need is the Lord Jesus Christ. Let me share with you the message God has given me for these people . . . Blah . . . blah . . . blah."

It was embarrassing. Once or twice my friend tried to inter-ject a question to give the discussion the semblance of an inter-view, but the preacher would have none of it. He was going like a machine gun until he ran out of ammunition.

A few months later I was not totally surprised to learn that minister had a complete nervous breakdown. He was not far from it the day I saw him at the interview.

The failure to listen to others can afflict people even when they mean well. A new member of our staff once pointed out that our weekly leadership planning meeting had become a talking session. Everyone was talking at the same time, and few were listening. It took an outsider to make us aware of this problem. At the next meeting, I announced that "starting this moment, we are going to talk one at a time, and we are going to listen to each other." Oh, if only it were that easy. I became a kind of traffic cop, holding up my hand to shut down conver-sations that were breaking out all over the room or to signal that someone was interrupting the speaker. No one meant to be disrespectful, but that was the result. We had to learn all over again how to listen to each other.

A Genuine Need

The starting point in learning to listen is to admit this is a gen-uine need in our ministry. Unfortunately, many of the Lord's servants will never make it to this point, holding that if God called them to speak, He must have called others to listen. Those who know me best will testify that I was born tainted by this original sin. (We used to say a talker was "vaccinated by a phonograph needle," but that metaphor is now lost to the ages.)

Pastor Robert Fisher tells how he learned the incredible power of listening as a ministerial student in college. Stymied in his attempts to become a good conversationalist, even after memorizing witty remarks and funny stories, one day he read that in order to become effective in this art, one must first become a good listener. This was a new thought to him. Since he was planning to hitchhike across the state the next day to visit a friend, he decided to test the theory and listen to everyone who picked him up.

The first man to give Fisher a ride soon began talking about his life, his business, and his family. Occasionally, the ministerial student would respond or ask a question. The man enjoyed talking so much that he kept deciding to take Fisher farther and farther until eventually he had driven the entire three hundred miles and delivered him at his friend's doorstep. During all this time, not once had the man even asked the name of his rider or anything about his life. As he let Fisher out of the car, he said, "Young man, you are one of the finest conversationalists I've ever met."[2]

As Robert Fisher discovered, the person who learns to listen is well on the way to becoming a great conversationalist. He is building a foundation for becoming a friend, a counselor, and a wise person. On the other hand, the one who never learns to hear others will always be a poor conversationalist and consequently will have few friends. If he is a minister of the gospel, he will find his "deafness" seriously limits his work for the Lord. He will be unable to sympathize with the hurting, will give poor counsel to his members, will not learn from the wisdom of others, and may in time become a one-man show destined for failure in dealing with people. Simply admitting "I need to learn to listen" will not win the race, but it will get you to the starting gate.

A pastor called a young person up to the pulpit and said, "I want to ask you some questions."

"What do we call a tree that has acorns?" he began.

"An oak," the youth responded.

"Right. Now, what do we call a funny story?"

"A joke."

"Right again. Now, what do we call the sound made by a frog?"

"A croak."

"And what do we call the white of an egg?"

"The yolk."

"Wrong. The yolk is the yellow. But thanks for being a good sport and helping me make my point. Today's sermon is on listening."

When my family lived in North Carolina, it seemed that every other car carried a personalized license plate. Frequently, at the traffic light I would ask the driver what his tag meant. One fellow's plate read "WHUUT?" At the intersection I called over to him, "What does your tag mean?" He said, "Whuut?" I said, "Never mind." This fellow wore his poor listening skill as a badge. Ideally, he is the exception, and the rest of us do a better job of hearing one another.

John Drakeford insisted that listening is the ultimate communication skill and the most profound motivational, counseling, and conversational technique. But he added, "It is generally overlooked."[3]

One evening a young lady dined with British Prime Minister William Gladstone. The next night she happened to be seated beside former Prime Minister Benjamin Disraeli. When someone later asked her impression of these two leaders of Britain, she replied, "When I left Mr. Gladstone, I thought he was the cleverest man in England. When I left Mr. Disraeli, I thought I was the cleverest woman in England."[4] The writer who cites this incident does not say, but I would hazard a guess that the first man was a great talker and the second a great listener.

Listening Is Work

On those occasions when we are hearing pleasant music or complimentary words or the laughter of a child, listening can be pure joy. I recall a time when my wife and I joined our friends Jim and Darlene Graham at an Everly Brothers open-air concert in a huge park in Atlanta. The songs we heard that day were the background music of our youth, and on the way home we laughed and sang them all over again. That was nearly twenty years ago, and I recall it like it was yesterday. Listening can be one of life's highest pleasures.

But focusing on others in order to listen intently also can be hard work. Listening is a skill to be developed, a discipline to be learned, a means to an end, an affirmation to the one speaking, an education to the hearer, and an invisible line connecting the two people involved in the conversation. Listening requires the whole person—the organ of hearing to take in the words, the brain to make sense of them, the eyes to connect with the other person, and the body to receive the nonverbal portions of the talk and to react appropriately.

One day recently, I spent four hours counseling with some friends on a family issue. In the afternoon I met with two of them for a couple of hours, and that night with the others. By the third hour I was growing weary. By the fourth I had to force myself to sit still, to pay attention, and to try to grasp what I was hearing. Listening is hard work.

Work to Be Silent

Driving across town to the monthly gathering of pastors, I began to think about the next two hours. If I held to my usual pattern, I would talk too much and not listen, then feel bad all afternoon as a result. "Lord," I prayed, "give me the gift of silence." I had never asked the Lord for this gift, but it certainly seemed a logical request.

Later on the way back to the office, I said, "Lord, I did it again. I dominated conversations with other ministers and did not listen. I wish You had answered my prayer and given me the gift of silence." At that moment the Lord spoke to my heart and said, "Silence is not a gift. It's a work."

That was a wonderful insight, one that applies both to silence and to listening. These are not divinely bestowed gifts to be received as a result of a prayer of faith, but works to be achieved by intense effort and self-discipline. It is no accident that *silent* and *listen* are composed of the same letters, for they are two sides of the same coin. Only the silent will listen. Only the silent can listen.

My friend Walter Moore made an observation about silence. He repaired business machines for local companies. One evening quitting time arrived, and the employees left Walter alone in an office. That's when he noticed for the first time that the company provided piped-in music. No one had been able to hear it for the noise.

The three great enemies of silence and listening are hurry, crowds, and noise. The cure for hurry is stillness, the remedy for crowds is solitude, and the opposite of noise is silence. Our intimacy with God is nurtured only in stillness, solitude, and silence. In Mark 6:31, the Lord Jesus said to His disciples to get away from the crowd for a while so they could rest.

President John Adams once remarked that the trait of George Washington he most admired was his silence. An inveterate talker, Adams found himself drawn to this man who had disciplined himself to be quiet. As one afflicted by the same disease, I frequently find myself praying Psalm 141:3, "Set a watch, O LORD, before my mouth; keep the door of my lips."

A church member who had heard me say that I start every day praying that verse once gave it to me in calligraphy and beautifully framed. But she had misunderstood me. I did not mean to imply this was my favorite verse, only that I pray it repeatedly out of recognition of a great weakness. (The framed verse is collecting dust in a closet somewhere.)

Wayne Oates once watched a friend grow camellias in a part of the country where they were not native. He observed how she spent time and energy and great effort to grow the flowers on their terms and not hers. Using his observation as an analogy, he added that silence is not native to us. Consequently, we have to be eager to nourish it.[5] The seventeenth-century philosopher Blaise Pascal said, "All the evils of life have fallen upon us because men will not sit quietly in a room."[6]

Learning to Listen Actively

During forty years of ministry in the church, I have learned that effective pastoral counseling involves four activities: active listening, silent praying, gentle probing, and timely teaching. None of them is easy; active listening may be the hardest.

"Active" listening refers to the way we take in information that has special meaning to us. Before taking me for a ride in an Air Force jet, the pilot spent an hour briefing me on the operation of my parachute and the ejection seat. I assure you that everything inside me was on full alert. I knew that my life might well depend on how well I listened that day. "Passive" listening is the way we receive information that means nothing to us. As an example, think of the last time you read the newspaper with the television going in the background. Did you remember much of either what you heard or read?

In order to learn to listen actively to others, there are some steps we can take. The good news is they work. On the other hand, we have to repeat them every day of our lives.

Job 1: Turn off your engine. Quiet your spirit. Do not talk. Relax. Still your body. Stop the drumming fingers, the chewing gum, and the swinging leg. Put both feet on the floor and breathe deeply.

Job 2: Focus on the other person. Look her in the eye. Keep your eyes on him. Do not let your mind and eyes wander around the room or check to see who has entered. Ignore the clock. Give your complete, undivided attention to the one talking. Turn your body in his or her direction.

Job 3: Remove the barriers. Get out from behind the desk. Arrange the chairs in your office so that both you and the speaker may sit close enough, but not too close. A friend tells me that her doctor has two chairs for visitors, one close to him and one not so close. The client gets to choose where to sit.

Job 4: Stifle the urge to speak. Your visitor says something that prompted a great thought or a pertinent story inside you. The urge to tell it is building like magma inside a volcano. You feel you will burst if you don't get it out. But—you won't. So don't. You may want to keep a note pad in your lap and write down that thought to be shared later.

Job 5: Use the lulls in the conversation. Professional interviewers, those who do it well—I'm thinking of Larry King or

Oprah here—know that when they are quiet with no tendency to rush, the speaker relaxes and talks more freely. When the speaker pauses in the conversation, the interviewer remains still and does not rush to fill the void. As a result, frequently the person will go on to say more than he had intended. Lawyers and prosecutors have developed this technique to an art form. The minister needs the skill in order to receive everything the visitor has come to share.

Job 6: Ask the Holy Spirit to help you love that person. When I asked a pastor with great listening skills for his secret, he thought a long time before answering. Finally he said, "I guess it's because I love them, and they know it." There's no substitute for genuine caring.

Job 7: Let your face join the conversation. Somewhere I picked up a story of a fellow who stood by a swollen river waiting for someone to give him a ride to the other side. Travelers came and went until finally the man walked up to a horseman and asked him for a ride. When they got to the other side, he thanked the horseman, who rode away. Someone said, "Do you know who that was?" "No," he said. "That was Thomas Jefferson. Why did you ask him of all people for a ride?" The man said, "I did not ask him because he was Mr. Jefferson. I asked him because he had a 'yes' face." We all know people whose countenance seems to warn others away. We who would minister in Jesus' name must practice showing people the same grace and acceptance our Savior showed those who came to Him.

A man once poured out a litany of troubles and fears to his psychiatrist. When he finished, the doctor instructed him to take a day off and go to the beach. Then he gave his patient an envelope and told him to open it once he got there. Next day, the man drove to the beach. He chose a secluded place and opened the envelope. Inside he found a small piece of white paper with the words "Listen carefully." That day he heard new sounds: the waves beating upon the shore, the wind whistling through the palms, and the birds singing. A moment of silence became for him a moment of great revelation.[7]

Listen carefully. Revelation awaits on every side.

CHAPTER 4

Being Assertive

Margaret F. Williamson

Communication styles are generally described in three categories: passive, aggressive, and assertive. Of the three, the assertive style is least understood or appreciated by many Christians. Christians tend to overlook assertiveness, assuming that passive and aggressive styles are the only possible options. Why have we opted to overlook assertiveness as a legitimate style of communication? To answer that question, we should learn more about all three of these communication styles.

A *passive* or *non-assertive* style denies the communicator's right to express his or her own thoughts and feelings. A passive communicator generally thinks that his or her thoughts and opinions do not matter.

An *aggressive* style describes a communicator who attacks anyone who has a different thought or opinion. An aggressive communicator tends to express his or her needs and desires at the expense of what others need or want to say.

An *assertive* style affirms the communicator's rights to personal thoughts and feelings while still respecting the thoughts and feelings of others. An assertive communicator is able to state his or her position positively, confidently, and persistently. Most important, assertive behavior demonstrates respect for the communicator, for others, and for the communicator's value system.

All three communication styles have merit, and each is appropriate at different times. Why, then, do Christians tend to avoid assertive behavior? In a recent seminary class discussion on assertion, students overwhelmingly agreed that Christ modeled only passive behavior and that He was never assertive. The students' impression of the concept of assertiveness was negative. For that reason, they could not accept that Christ ever became assertive. Considering examples of Christ's behavior, however, can help us to place assertiveness in a more positive light.

Jesus' Communication Style

Jesus demonstrated an assertive style early in His life. Luke records a conversation Jesus had with Mary and Joseph when He was twelve. On a visit to Jerusalem, Jesus became separated from His parents. They had left town on the journey home before they realized Jesus was missing. They returned to Jerusalem and spent three days looking for Him. When they finally found Him, they were obviously exasperated! Mary's frustration was evident by her complaint to Jesus that she and Joseph had looked for Him everywhere. Jesus' response was direct and simple, and it communicated His personal values eloquently. Jesus told them in no uncertain terms that He had to be in His Father's house and about His Father's business.[1]

Is this an assertive response? Consider how Jesus could have responded. A passive response would have been something like, "I'm sorry I got separated. I'll never do it again." Such a response would have denied that He was following His Father. An aggressive response would have been more defensive, something like, "What do you care what I do? I'm almost grown, and I don't have to answer to you for My actions." Again, such a response would have been inappropriate. His assertive response demonstrated His certainty that He was doing what He was supposed to be doing. He took a stand for His actions and His behavior, yet He respected the thoughts and opinions of Mary and Joseph.

Consider also Jesus' encounter with the scribes and the Pharisees who brought the woman caught in adultery before Him.[2] Jewish law required that the woman be stoned for her actions. The religious leaders asked Jesus what He thought they should do with her. He could have chosen a passive response and watched without interference while the sentence of death was carried out, or He could have been aggressive and argued with the scribes and Pharisees about their misinterpretation of the Jewish law. Jesus chose, however, to be assertive. He responded by telling the religious leaders that the person who had no sin could cast the first stone at her.

Why is this an assertive response? First, Jesus' response did not reflect that He was angry or argumentative. Second, His response was non-judgmental. He did not accuse the woman or the people in the crowd of wrongdoing. He simply called for them to evaluate their own lives. Third, His response was based on Kingdom values. He believed in the worth of every individual and that everyone could be forgiven. In just a few assertive words, Jesus provided a standard of how people should be treated.

Consider yet another example from the Bible. Jesus' encounter with Pilate demonstrated His assertiveness.[3] Jesus had been arrested, brought to the high priest Caiaphas, and then taken to Pilate. Jesus chose not to defend Himself to His accusers, but He wasn't being passive. Later, when Jesus was questioned personally by Pilate, He spoke truthfully, completely, and without malice. He was in control of His words and His actions. Jesus' behavior must have been troubling to Pilate. Pilate demonstrated his frustration by pointing out to Jesus that he had the authority to have Jesus crucified.

Jesus could have chosen to respond to Pilate with a passive response of silence. He could have chosen an aggressive response by accusing Pilate of wrongdoing and by trying to challenge Pilate's sense of power. Instead, He responded by asserting that Pilate had no authority over Him unless God Himself wanted it.

What makes this an assertive response? Jesus did not give up the control of His words and His actions, even though He made no apology and no defense before Pilate. He remained true to His understanding of His call from God, and He didn't attack Pilate in the process.

Of course, other examples from the ministry of Jesus could be considered. The selected examples provide a foundational understanding that Jesus modeled an assertive communication style throughout His ministry.

Types of Behavior

The idea of being assertive is not always viewed positively in our society. Perhaps the characteristics of assertive behavior are confused with those of aggressive behavior. Robert Bolton wrote that assertion skills "enable you to maintain respect, satisfy your needs, and defend your rights without dominating, manipulating, abusing, or controlling others."[4] How can assertion render such positive results and be so misunderstood at the same time? To answer that question, consider in detail three types of behavior: passive behavior, aggressive behavior, and assertive behavior.

Passive Behavior

Passive behavior can be described as "self-denying; inhibited; hurt, anxious; allows others to choose; [and] does not achieve desired goals."[5] A passive person tends to refrain from expressing his or her own feelings.[6] Ultimately, a passive person who doesn't express his or her thoughts and feelings allows others to treat him or her with disregard.[7]

Often, people choose passive behavior in an attempt to keep the peace or not to cause problems. As Lange and Jakubowski have suggested, the goal of such non-assertive behavior "is to appease others and to avoid conflict at any cost."[8]

Unfortunately, passive behavior can encourage misuse. A passive person communicates, "I don't matter. You can take advantage of me."[9] Additionally, not only does a passive person demonstrate a lack of self-respect, but he or she also "indicates a lack of respect for the other person, too . . . [by implying] the other is too fragile to handle confrontation" or handle his or her share of the load.[10]

A non-assertive person experiences some advantages from

his or her passive behavior. Bolton mentioned some of them: a sense of comfort, the approval of others, the absence of risk, and the avoidance of conflict.[11] However, such a person pays a high price for such behavior by nurturing relationships that are less satisfying, generating disgust, repressing anger, surrendering emotional control, and giving up self.[12]

Six reasons can be offered for why people choose non-assertive behavior instead of assertive behavior. First, as discussed previously, people mistake assertive behavior for aggressive behavior. Second, people mistake non-assertive behavior as more polite than assertive behavior. Third, people refuse to accept and act upon their personal rights—the right to express personal feelings and opinions, the right to stand up for themselves, and the right to meet their own needs. Fourth, people become anxious about facing negative reactions or consequences if they use assertive behavior. Fifth, people mistake non-assertive behavior as being more helpful to others than assertive behavior. Sixth, people choose not to use assertive behavior because they simply do not have the necessary skills.[13]

Aggressive Behavior

The word *aggression* is defined as "the practice of making attacks or encroachments; . . . hostile, injurious, or destructive behavior or outlook, esp. when caused by frustration."[14] People who demonstrate aggressive behavior tend to overpower their opponents in order to get what they want.[15]

An aggressive person "accomplishes goals at the expense of others."[16] For an aggressive person, "winning is insured by humiliating, degrading, belittling, or overpowering other people so that they become weaker and less able to express and defend their needs and rights."[17]

Some psychologists talk about another pattern of behavior that is actually a part of aggressive behavior, referring to it as either indirect aggression or passive aggression. At times, aggressive behavior uses passive or non-confrontation responses. Similarly, an indirect aggressive person can be friendly in person while attacking or undermining people when they are not present.[18]

Being aggressive certainly has advantages. Aggressive people can usually get what they want, they can usually protect themselves, and they can exert considerable control over others.[19] On the other hand, aggressive people pay a terrible price for such behavior. For instance, they live with the fear that they will lose control, be shamed, and be alienated from others.[20]

Five reasons can be cited for why people choose aggressive behavior. First, people who are afraid of attack or even feeling vulnerable can choose aggressive behavior to combat these feelings of powerlessness and threat. Second, people who have demonstrated non-assertive behavior often turn to aggressive behavior when they feel their rights have been compromised. Third, people who have unresolved emotional experiences tend to overreact by using aggressive behavior. Fourth, people mistakenly believe that aggressive behavior is the only way of getting what they want. Fifth, aggressive people may have received positive reinforcement of their aggressive behavior from family members or others.[21]

Assertive Behavior

Assertive behavior can be described as "standing up for personal rights and expressing thoughts, feelings, and beliefs in direct, honest, and appropriate ways which do not violate another person's rights.[22] Alberti and Emmons identify some helpful characteristics of assertive behavior. These characteristics show that assertive people have a healthy respect for themselves, for others, and for the situations in which assertion is appropriate.[23]

People who demonstrate assertive behavior receive some benefits. First, assertive people like themselves. They tend to feel better about who they are than submissive or aggressive people. Second, assertive behavior leads to more gratifying relationships. Third, assertive people are able to get what they want from life.

However, negative consequences of assertive behavior exist

as well. They include "disruptions in one's life, the pain associated with honest and caring confrontation, and the arduous personal struggle involved in altering one's own habitual behaviors."[24]

Steps to Assertive Behavior

In the previous description of passive behavior, the observation was made that people choose not to use assertive behavior because they lack assertion skills. Alberti and Emmons offer an approach for developing assertion skills. Their approach includes a series of seventeen steps. By following each of the steps, a person is engaged in a sequence of important actions like introspection, goal-setting, concentration, evaluation, modeling, and accountability.[25]

Although the approach can be helpful, it appears to be somewhat cumbersome due to the extended number of steps involved in it. Another process collapses Alberti and Emmons's approach into four steps. First, realize where changes are needed and believe in your rights. Second, figure out appropriate ways of asserting yourself in each specific situation that concerns you. Third, practice giving assertive responses. Fourth, try being assertive in real-life situations.[26]

Assertive people are willing to stand up for their own rights as well as the rights of others. Christians, especially ministers, can improve their abilities to relate to others and influence their communities by developing assertive behavior skills. You have a choice in any situation to respond passively, aggressively, or assertively. It is possible to change between these three styles as situations change. Therefore, do not shortchange yourself by using only passive or aggressive behavior. Assertive behavior can be included as a legitimate communication style for ministers.

CHAPTER 5

Forgiving

Argile Smith

I know what you're thinking. Forgiving someone shouldn't really be classified as an interpersonal relationship skill. For some people, forgiving doesn't seem to fit neatly into the same category as communicating, listening, or managing conflict. It's more like praying, tithing, witnessing, and meditating on God's Word. Like these and other disciplines we practice in our walk with Jesus, forgiving helps us nurture the character of Christ in our lives.

I agree that forgiving is a spiritual discipline. At the same time, however, it includes interpersonal relationship skills. The mandate to forgive people goes to the heart of our walk with Christ as His disciples. In turn, our relationship with the Lord prompts us to see our way clear to go the distance in forgiving others who have hurt us. The actual process of forgiving people takes us through some pretty rough waters. Moving through the rapids or even staying afloat requires us to put into practice some basic "forgiveness survival" skills in our interpersonal relationships.

Survival Skill #1: Make the Decision to Forgive

Forgiving others requires us to make a difficult decision. Will we make up our mind to forgive, or will we just try it for a while to see what happens? Will we be resolute in our decision, or will we vacillate between yes and no?

James, the half-brother of Jesus and author of the Bible book bearing his name, shows the value of making up our mind. In James 1:5 he encourages Christians to ask God for the wisdom we need to rejoice in our struggles. Almost in the same breath, though, he warns us to make up our mind about putting God's wisdom into practice once we receive it. If we do, we will be rock steady in the face of the challenges that will always accompany the living out of God's wisdom. If we don't, His wisdom will be lost on us like a floating flower atop turbulent water getting sucked under the waves.

Forgiveness is always a wise move, as we will see later. If we resolve to put it into practice, we will eventually be able to celebrate its triumph. If we take an "I'm going to wait and see how it turns out first" attitude, we won't be able to see it through. Like any wise move God prompts us to make, we can't afford to waver in our decision to act on it.

Paul helps us strengthen our resolve to forgive in 2 Corinthians 2:5-11. In this passage of his letter to the Corinthian church, he brings up a situation in which a person in the congregation has done something that hurt everyone. Now the congregation needs to forgive him.

As you read his appeal, you can pick out four formidable reasons to practice the hard but necessary work of forgiving people who have hurt us. First, it's an act of obedience.[1] Unfortunately as disciples of Jesus we don't have the privilege of picking and choosing the ways in which we show our obedience to Him. He has given us clear instruction on the matter of forgiving others. For instance, in Matthew 6:12 He implies our willingness to forgive others as we ask Him to forgive us. In Matthew 6:14-15 He goes on to make it crystal clear: Kingdom citizens are obligated to be forgiving people.

In His instruction about forgiving others, Jesus offered no exceptions, no qualifiers, and no loopholes. Perhaps that's what Peter was looking for when he asked Jesus how many times he had to forgive someone who hurt him.[2] We still ponder the same question: how many times do we allow one person to hurt us before we give up on forgiveness? And Jesus' answer to Peter's inquiry still gets stuck in our throats at times. With His answer, Jesus made it clear to Peter and to us. His disciples can never say that our well of forgiveness has run dry. Therefore, we can't set limits on how many times we will forgive someone.

Jesus told us to forgive others. It's not a suggestion but a command. We don't have a choice in the matter. If we intend to obey Him completely, we have to forgive.

Second, we make up our minds to forgive because of the Christians who are watching us. Ministers have a unique privilege and responsibility to live out their relationship with Christ in the presence of folks in the church. In turn, church members follow the example we set for them. In a way, it's all a part of being a mentor or, to use another term, a disciple-maker.

Paul knew about the value of his example. Throughout his letters he called attention to the model he set for the believers in the churches. And he challenged the people to follow his example in their walk with Christ. To the Corinthian Christians he wrote that he had forgiven the person who had caused the church so much pain. When he did it, he added, he had the congregation in mind.[3] He knew they would be watching him. If he could forgive, then perhaps they could too.

In our ministries we cannot underestimate the value of our example. The people in the churches watch us as much as they listen to us. The more they see us live out the precepts of Christ, the more they will be encouraged to do the same thing. By the same token, if they hear us talk about forgiving others, but they see us refusing to forgive someone who has injured us, they will be left in a dilemma. Usually, they resolve the dilemma by doing as we do and not as we say. Or they may follow our example to the extreme. Just like us, they will talk about forgiving, but they will never do it themselves.

When it comes to the tough decision to forgive, our example must correlate with our instruction. For the sake of the people in our congregations who watch us, we have no other choice but to model a forgiving heart. To press the issue even further, consider not only the people in the church, but also the people who live with you in your home. Your spouse and your children deserve to see you demonstrate a willingness to forgive. The consistency you exhibit between precept and example will help them grow up with a good model of how to walk with God to the point that you can forgive other people.

Third, we forgive because of Christ.[4] Paul set the example for the Corinthian congregation by forgiving the person who had hurt them. Apparently Paul himself had been hurt. Yet in spite of the pain he suffered, he led the way by practicing forgiveness. By now you may have the opinion that the Lord put Paul on a different spiritual plane than the rest of us. How else could he so readily extend a forgiving hand to someone whose actions had apparently broken his heart?

No. God didn't place Paul on a pedestal and give him something He didn't give us. The Lord in us enables us to have the same potential as Paul to forgive people. Paul wasn't prompted to forgive because he ate a super-spiritual energy bar that God cooked up for him alone. He was moved to forgive because he remembered how much it cost Jesus to forgive him.

Think about it for a minute. When Luke introduced us to Paul in Acts 7:58, his name was Saul, and he was an observer as an angry mob of religious leaders murdered Stephen, who was being stoned simply because he was a Christian. A religious zealot himself, Paul endorsed the murder and even added his own brand of terrorism to the ardent quest to rid the world of Jesus' followers. According to Acts 9, that's what put him on the road to Damascus, and that's where he met Jesus. As Luke told the story, in a few days Paul himself became a follower of Christ. There in Damascus, Jesus melted the ice of Paul's hatred and fired up his heart with God's love.

In other words, Jesus forgave him. For the rest of his life, Paul could not get very far from the way Jesus forgave him. As a tribute of his love of his Savior, he lived out Christ's forgiveness in his relationships with others. Jesus said to a cynical religious leader that people love in proportion to the extent to which they have been forgiven.[5] When it came to people who sinned against Jesus, Paul knew that he himself stood at the front of the line. He had tried to do a great deal of harm to Jesus. Yet Jesus forgave him and even called him to be an apostle. Paul knew that he had been forgiven of a sin debt he couldn't pay. That's why he loved Jesus so much, and that's why he was able to forgive those who sinned against him.

For some reason you may be thinking that what happened to you exempts you from forgiving the person or people who hurt you. The pain inflicted on you by someone else may give you justification for passing on the option to forgive. If that's the case, write down on a piece of paper the wrongs that were inflicted on you. When you are finished, roll up the paper, place it in the nail-pierced palm of Jesus' hand, and ask for permission to be excused from forgiving. If you are like most Christians, you can't do it.

The cross of Jesus casts a long, haunting shadow over the self-styled altar of our reluctance to forgive. When we recall what He has done for us in forgiving us, we can't justify our unwillingness to forgive others. Our love for Jesus leaves us with no other choice. We must forgive, because He forgave us.

Fourth, we forgive because of the evil one.[6] Paul implied that the Corinthian Christians knew about the extent to which the devil could influence them. Under the right circumstances, he could compel them to say and do things that would disgust them later. He could trap them with their own thoughts, emotions, and actions, turning them into far less than the unique people God intended them to be in Christ.

When it comes to forgiving, you have probably seen the devil convince a person that he or she has a right to refuse to forgive. He may have even convinced you yourself that God will exempt you from forgiving the person who injured you, insulted you, or scarred you deeply.

If you have fallen for his lie, excuse yourself from the hard decision to forgive and see what happens. If you are like most other people, you may be able to live with the pain for a while, but not forever. Before you know it, your pain will have turned into anger and resentment will heat up into a kind of seething bitterness. After a while it will boil up, rising to the surface through what you think, then what you say, then what you do. In due time, the bitterness will imprison you. Eventually it will destroy you, and along the way it will gradually and sometimes imperceptibly siphon all the life out of you. And there you will be—a shell of the person God meant for you to become.

And the whole miserable process begins with the devil. With his sweet lie that you don't have to take forgiveness seriously, he can poison you for the rest of your life. So don't swallow it! Granted, some of the cruel injuries some people inflict on others defy comprehension. If you have been victimized by such horrible injustices, you may consider forgiveness to be out of the question. Although it sounds tough, forgiveness is the only way to deal with what happened to you so you can be liberated to nurture healthy relationships with the Lord, other people, and even yourself. The devil has already ruined too many lives. You can choose not to be one of his next victims.

Survival Skill #2: Give Forgiveness Some Time

Susan had no choice but to forgive her mother. Called to ministry, she had some serious concerns about whether the injuries her mom had inflicted on her soul would get in her way as she served the Lord. She could already tell, for example, that she was having a difficult time respecting some of the older women in her church. For the sake of her calling, she knew she must not give the devil an opportunity to ruin her life. So she chose to forgive.

She began to pray, "Father, I forgive my mother for everything she did to me. I don't hold it against her." When she finished praying, nothing happened. The pain was still there, and so was her mother, oblivious to what she had done to Susan. The whole episode confused her. Why had nothing happened?

Susan had not factored in an important variable in forgiving people: time. Because we tend to ignore it too, we foster three misconceptions about how forgiveness really works.

The first misconception involves the connection between forgiveness and reconciliation. Forgiveness starts with a decision based on biblical insights like 1 Corinthians 2, and hopefully it ends with restored relationships. The time lapse between deciding to forgive and seeing broken relationships restored can often be measured in minutes. Sometimes, however, it unfortunately can span many years. For that reason you have to give forgiveness time.

Some people think that forgiving and reconciling are the same thing. But they aren't. Forgiveness means putting away the injuries one person has inflicted on another. Reconciliation means tearing down walls between people. As you can see, forgiveness is the first critical step toward tearing down the walls in broken relationships. But a great deal of work has to be done before those walls can actually come down.

The two words—*forgiveness* and *reconciliation*—aren't synonyms. They are more like two cities located on the same map. Although close together, some traveling has to be done in order to get from one place to another. Relationally speaking, going from forgiveness to reconciliation may turn out to be quite a journey. So be sure to allow for plenty of traveling time.

The trip toward reconciliation may be uphill all the way. Sometimes the road will be blocked altogether, and you will never be able to get there. For instance, suppose you have escaped a relationship that continues to have the potential for danger because of the abuse or neglect associated with it. As much as you may want to restore the relationship, you can't. You have no choice but to accept the roadblock and what it means. You can still forgive, but that's all you can do.

Not being able to reconcile may break your heart. Being able to forgive, however, will take you a long way toward healing it.

The second misconception has to do with forgiving and forgetting. The truth is that only God can truly forgive and forget. Scripture passages like Isaiah 43:25 and Jeremiah 31:34 leave us with the distinct impression that God can put our sins out of His mind, never to remember them again. His willingness to forget our sin shows the depth of His loving grace toward His people.

But Scripture doesn't teach us that forgetting always follows forgiving people who have hurt us. The Lord doesn't leave us with the impression that the evidence of genuine forgiveness is a loss of memory. When we forgive, we can't necessarily let go of the memory. We can only decide to let go of the pain that accompanies it.

In order to let go of the pain, however, we need God's help. It is not something we can do by ourselves. When we utter the words of forgiveness, we depend on the Lord to help our heart to live out our utterance. In time, we find ourselves not being able to remember the pain, because God has helped us to get rid of it. We may always remember the incident, but the process of forgiving helps us to forget how much it hurt us.

The third misconception is that forgiveness always has an effect on the person who is forgiving. Do you remember the story of Susan and her mother? She assumed that her act of forgiveness would make an impact on her mom. She was almost certain that her mother would respond by doing something that would show her remorse for the pain she had inflicted on her daughter.

It didn't happen that way. Furthermore, it doesn't often happen that way.

When we forgive people who have hurt us, we don't always experience the joy of having them reciprocate by saying they regret what they have done to us. If they do, the road to reconciliation certainly gets shorter and less difficult to travel. Many stories of forgiveness, however, have less than happy endings.

Then, you may be asking, why should I forgive? Because forgiving has its own rewards. You forgive because it's the right thing to do, not because it will have an effect on the person who hurt you. The persons who caused you pain may not even know that you have forgiven them. Or if they know, they may not care.

But you will know. You will know that by forgiving you will live like an obedient follower of Christ. And you will know that you will not become a slave to the bitterness that so often accompanies being victimized by injustice. Furthermore, you will know that the time you will take to live out your decision to forgive will be time well spent.

Forgiving others is a spiritual discipline that requires us put to work some basic skills. Two of them have been offered for your consideration: making a decision to forgive, and managing the misconceptions about forgiving. By no means does this short list exhaust the possibilities when it comes to working through the actual process of forgiving someone who has hurt you.

But perhaps it's a good start.

PART II

Your Relationship with Your Family

CHAPTER 6

Rewriting Your Family Story

Philip A. Coyle and Cara Cochran

Everyone loves a good story—or so the saying goes. What most of us do not realize is that the events of our lives create a story that is unique for each of us. Lives make sense only in the context of relationships. From the beginning this principle is seen as part of God's creation. Relationships give meaning to living; relationships generate emotion, and emotion embeds memories. Our family stories are the interpretations drawn from encounters within these relationships. The events that trigger strong emotions produce stronger stories. In time, the memories become a unique story, an interpretation of the actual event that triggered the original emotion. The interpretations triggered from emotional events or from a series of common experiences become a pattern, a filter for interpreting future experiences.

Family Style and Family Story

From early childhood on, we seek to identify ourselves in some meaningful way. Every encounter is assigned a meaning; these meanings combine and begin to define our identity. The framework of our personal stories—our core beliefs about ourselves, our world, our future—is constructed early in our lives and primarily through the numerous experiences within our family. Our identity is our life story. All relationships have an impact on the people involved. Of primary importance is our family of origin, or the family in which we grew up. Every family has a unique style or way of functioning. Even after we reach adulthood, these relationships and the unique styles of our families continue to have an impact on our lives.

This process of drawing meaning from life's experiences and developing an efficient cognitive pattern to interpret future events helps us adapt to a complex world. When an individual is raised in a healthy home environment, these cognitive patterns of interpretation enable the person to take risks, experience intimacy with others, adjust to losses and successes, solve problems, and accept and receive love. When an individual is raised in an unhealthy environment, the cognitive patterns of interpretation hinder these developments. Instead the cognitive patterns stray into compensatory structures enabling the person to defend, deny, dissociate, or rationalize an otherwise intolerable set of experiences. Exposure to a healthy family does not protect the personality from faulty thinking. Even in the healthiest, most loving of families, there is the potential to misinterpret messages and make them a harmful part of one's core belief system.

Messages drawn from parental statements or actions, significant losses, ongoing neglect, cultural or racial disparity, peer group behavior, and the like can produce irrational core beliefs. Enmeshed families, characterized by overinvolvement, extreme loyalty, and loss of individuality, tend to produce specific core beliefs in their children. Core beliefs among members of enmeshed families have themes such as "My worth is based on my performance," "I must please people to be liked," "The world is dangerous, and only my family is to be trusted," and "I must never be abandoned; therefore, I will do whatever it takes to stay attached."

At the other extreme, disengaged families are characterized by underinvolvement, lack of intimacy between family members, lack of loyalty and sense of belonging, and a skewed sense of independence. These families often produce children with a different set of core beliefs. Children from disengaged families tend to develop beliefs such as "I cannot trust anyone,"

"People are to be used for my personal advantage," "Intimacy is to be avoided," and "Meaning in life has little to do with relationships."

Families characterized by abuse or neglect frequently send their children conflicting messages about love and acceptance. These children develop beliefs that help them "make sense" of their parents' actions, beliefs such as "I deserve punishment," "I must be unlovable," "I will never do anything right," and "God must not hear me."

Children develop behavioral strategies to compensate for painful beliefs. These strategies are attempts to avoid reexperiencing the pain that comes when the old beliefs are triggered. However, in time the strategies often insure only that the core beliefs will be strengthened. For example, a sexual abuse victim may engage in promiscuous behavior as a young adult. Initially the numerous involvements prove to her that she is lovable and acceptable. Yet, eventually the behaviors themselves lead her to conclude that "My worth is based on pleasing others; I am loved only as a means to be used by another."

Jimmy's Story

Jimmy was a boy who had developed his worldview and his core beliefs about himself based upon a family whose style was enmeshed and chaotic. Jimmy had been in state custody for more than three years. He did not understand why his parents relinquished their rights and, in his words, "gave me to the state of Louisiana." One day he found his teacher's car keys on her desk. He took the keys and decided to go for a ride from New Orleans to Baton Rouge. Jimmy was only twelve and could barely see above the dashboard to drive. Yet, he found a way: being self-reliant, he took the car. He had almost arrived in Baton Rouge before the car ran out of gas. Being a survivor, he saw a sign on the road that read "Jimmy Swaggart Bible College" and hatched a plan. He found change in the car's ashtray and made a call to the college. Someone came, and he was able to convince the person to provide gas and some cash for his trip. Being raised in an enmeshed, conflictual family, he had acquired a number of skills to survive in times of crisis. We eventually found Jimmy about two weeks later; he now was in his third vehicle, this time a conversion van. We brought him back to New Orleans. In the next counseling session, I asked him where he was headed. He answered very directly, "I was trying to find my father." He paused awhile and with a hollow expression said, "but my father does not want to be found." He then began to express how he must have been such a disappointment to his father. He just wanted to show his father that he had changed and that he could be good now. The truth, however, was that Jimmy had always been a good kid; he made good grades, and he had never had any serious behavior problems. In fact, he personally had nothing to do with his removal from his parents' care. His parents were crack cocaine addicts and lost custody of Jimmy when he was nine. Jimmy's life with his parents during these first nine years was chaotic, unpredictable, and hostile. Jimmy's life story was devoid of much truth.

The larger truth that needs to be understood in Jimmy's story and in our own stories is that our Heavenly Father wants to be found by us! He is always available. He is portrayed in the Bible as the waiting father who runs to us from the distance that we have created to hug us upon our return. He throws a party and gives us a feast to celebrate our return.[1] God continually seeks intimacy with us. Without an understanding of God's nature and without a narrative that fully incorporates His love for us, we are destined to story our lives with deceit. If our story is incongruent with His story, then we will not have an honest history with which to construct our life narrative.

A Foundation of God's Grace

Even within the church family, people can develop false beliefs about themselves, beliefs based upon negative memories and incorrect messages rather than biblical truth. Within the church, people may mistakenly come to believe "I must be perfect or do things perfectly to be of any real worth," "I must work to earn God's love," or "I must put myself last in every situation in order to be a good Christian." Often the messages are implied rather than overt and are based on partial truth rather than the whole counsel of God's Word.

Each of us has had experiences that negatively affect our worldview. We each have a life story based upon the accumulation of our experiences. The story is not always accurate or valid. The story may have been prescribed by other people for their own personal gain. The core of the story may have been created from a dependent child's perspective and never reexamined for its validity and usefulness today. The story of our life can be changed; if the story is not valid, then rewriting the valid narrative will provide new freedom resulting from the truth.

Rewriting family stories may be particularly necessary for those who have suffered severe emotional, physical, and sexual abuse. Survivors of such abuse may find it extremely helpful to understand how they interpreted such negative experiences and what *incorrect* beliefs they may have developed out of painful emotional situations. Yet, even those who have not experienced abuse need to examine the narrative of our life.

So, how does one rewrite a family story? The good news is, as Scripture attests, that we have a choice in how we think about ourselves and our situations. Rewriting our story involves not only making a conscious choice to change the way we think, but also realizing how God sees us. Often, though we know *intellectually* that God loves us unconditionally, *emotionally* we may feel that we must work to earn His love. Learning to feel God's love for us means that we need to relax, to be still and know that He is God.[2] It's like trying to tread the water in a four-foot-deep pool. The incorrect messages we have learned in the past would say "Keep your feet up! Work harder! Paddle faster! You can do it if you try hard enough! You won't drown if you will just keep your feet up and tread faster!" The voice of reality, the true message we need to receive is "Relax. Put your feet down. The foundation is right there; you can simply stand."

The foundation is God's grace. Instead of working so hard to fight through the negative messages in our life, we can rest in God's unconditional love for us. If we could, even for just the briefest of moments, catch a glimpse of the enormity of God's love for us, we would be overwhelmed with the sense of peace and total acceptance. If only for a moment we could comprehend the extent of His love for us, our life would be changed forever. If only we could see God as He truly is, we would realize the truth of His love and have the freedom to rewrite the painful and inaccurate stories from our past.

Rewriting the Past

The facts of the past cannot be changed. What the events of the past mean to us, how we interpret them emotionally, can be changed! Changing the past begins by examining the events accurately. Often we blame ourselves for things that, as children, we had no power to control. No child can prevent an inebriated father from harming her or her mother. But often the message we hear says "If only I had . . ." While it wasn't possible for a child to change such a situation, the painful memories may result in beliefs of failure and helplessness.

Another aspect of examining events accurately means we must resist the temptation to see only the good and wonderful things in the past. Seeing only the positive aspects of the past may sound good and virtuous, but painful events will still affect us in the present whether they are acknowledged or not. Losses may need to be grieved. Anger over abuse may need to be expressed.

Rewriting the family story means seeing others in the story more realistically. Often, the situations that had the most impact were the result, not of intentional abuse or neglect, but of thoughtlessness or ignorance. Sometimes we need to look back and understand that those in our life who unintentionally caused hurt were themselves hurting. Perhaps they were under more stress than we understood at the time; maybe their parents used the same words or parenting techniques with them; older brothers and sisters may not have intended to be cruel; teachers possibly had no idea their methods of discipline caused humiliation. All of us are flawed and wounded in some way. To be able to empathize with those who unintentionally inflicted emotional pain is not intended to minimize the reality of the pain, but to understand that, in some situations, the motivation was not malicious.

Rewriting the family story also may mean forgiving those who hurt us. If we are able to empathize with them as hurting people who did the best they could under difficult circumstances, this forgiveness may not be so difficult. But what of those who *intentionally* inflicted horrible abuse? How can we forgive them? The ability to forgive requires that we understand what forgiveness is *not*. Forgiveness is *not* forgetting what happened. Forgiveness is *not* saying that what happened is somehow acceptable or less harmful than it was. Forgiveness does *not* mean that all the pain has gone away, nor does it necessarily mean the reconciliation of relationships. Forgiveness is the conscious choice to give up the right to bitterness and retaliation for the harmful behavior. Forgiveness means relinquishing the hold that another's actions have on our life. Forgiveness is an unearned gift that may or may not include reconciliation with the offender.

Forgiveness is also a process. In order to forgive, we must first acknowledge the reality and perhaps the enormity of what we are forgiving. Grieving the loss of innocence and a carefree childhood can take time and intentional emotional and spiritual work on the part of the survivor. However, at some point forgiveness can become a choice even when pain still remains. Choosing forgiveness means choosing no longer to be controlled by the past. Choosing forgiveness means having power over what messages we allow in our lives. The temptation to reclaim the bitterness and hatred that once controlled our thinking will undoubtedly recur. In those times, we must again choose forgiveness.[3]

Rewriting our family story may mean looking back to see what we learned from our families. Sometimes bad lessons are learned in a positive way; sometimes good lessons are learned in a negative way. Parentified children, who have had to take on adult roles due to dysfunctional family dynamics, may not learn how to play; but they may learn to be good managers and communicators. While this viewpoint may seem a grand Pollyanna rationalization, the truth is that some of our best traits come out of our most difficult situations. There is absolutely nothing good about intentional abuse! Those who survive abuse often do so out of their sheer strength of character. This strength of character should be celebrated in spite of the horrors that may have helped form it.

But what of the times when we need to rewrite stories for which *we* are the cause of the harm to ourselves and others? Again, we must begin to see ourselves as God does. To have God's perspective, we must be willing to forgive ourselves and be aware of the messages we place in our own minds. For some of us, this process may involve asking forgiveness of another person or doing something to rectify a wrong. We need to be as gentle with ourselves as Christ is—not ignoring our past sins and mistakes, but learning from them and moving forward.

Rewriting the Present and the Future

The wonderful thing about rewriting the family story from the past is that it gives us an even better chance of changing our present and future! The past is *not* doomed to repeat itself. One key to rewriting the present and future is to be aware of symptoms of negative emotions. Symptoms are a gift! While that may sound strange, think about symptoms in relation to our physical well-being. Painful symptoms alert us to a problem that could potentially cause more severe injury if not attended to. Likewise, emotional symptoms of anger, undue criticism, isolation, or inability to communicate in relationships may indicate that more serious problems may result if these matters are not dealt with. While the biblical admonition to "not let the sun go down on your anger"[4] is not necessarily meant to be taken literally, it does introduce the principle of dealing with emotional pain quickly before it builds to something that can cause more serious or even permanent harm to relationships.

Another way to rewrite the family story for the present and the future is to listen for the messages we tell ourselves. We all have automatic thoughts that constantly run through our minds like an ongoing monologue. We may remind ourselves of mundane things like "I've got to mail the bills tomorrow," and in emotional situations we may say very negative things to ourselves, such as "I can't believe I said something so stupid" or "He must really think I'm incompetent!" When such negative automatic thoughts occur, we should pay attention to the circumstances and the people involved. Sometimes writing down the thought and the situation is helpful. When we have time to distance ourselves from the situation, we can look at the thoughts more objectively: "What I said wasn't really stupid" or "He may not have liked my work, but he knows I'm really a good employee." Each of us is susceptible to cognitive distortions, or having thoughts that are not quite realistic about emotional situations. As we learn to be aware of these distortions, we gradually can change the messages we give to ourselves, in turn changing the family story in the present and in the future.

Rewriting the family story not only means getting rid of the harmful negative messages, but nourishing healthy, realistic messages. We all have abilities given to us by God. Acknowledging those abilities and our other positive traits can be a very helpful way to rewrite our family story. As we learn to see ourselves genuinely for the good of which we are capable, we learn to think more positively about ourselves. This more positive orientation does not mean that we should no longer pay attention to the negative and sinful things in our lives. As long as we live, we will need to pay attention to symptoms that need our attention and sins that need God's forgiveness. Acknowledging our abilities may sound prideful. Acknowledging abilities, in this context, means first of all acknowledging them to ourselves. We often deny the wonderful aspects of the people God created us to be. "I will praise thee; for I am fearfully and wonderfully made: marvellous are thy works; and that my soul knoweth right well" (Ps. 139:14). God not only made our bodies, but everything about us. Knowing our giftedness is not prideful unless we try to use it to make ourselves look better than others.

As we begin to nourish our minds, we should not ignore our bodies. What, you may ask, does physical health have to do with rewriting my family story? Everything! As we learn emotional messages in our families of origin, we also learn about how to take care of ourselves physically. Some families value exercise and a balanced diet; others do not. We develop health habits in our families of origin. Our physical well-being has an immediate impact on how we think. When we take care of ourselves physically, we think more clearly. Exercise is known to alleviate depression and raise self-esteem. As we come to see how God values us, we can begin to be proactive in valuing ourselves by becoming more intentional in our self-care.

For some of us, self-care may mean coming to the realization that we need to spend less time at work and more time with family. Some of us have become so addicted to the adrenaline rush of activity that we literally feel uncomfortable sitting down to have a leisurely conversation with a friend or family member. What message might this send—that the other person is not worthy of our time? Of course, that would not be what we mean to imply; but it is very possible that this is how the message is interpreted, particularly by young children. Rewriting some of these parts of our family story will have an immediate impact on the present and the future.

As we begin to nourish ourselves emotionally, spiritually, and physically, we also can begin to be more intentional about the messages we give to others. All of us have experienced having someone make an off-hand remark that either made or ruined our day. We also know how wonderful it feels to do something special for someone without any particular reason. Rewriting our family story is not just about the messages we receive; it is about the messages we give. Do we remember to say "I love you," "Thank you," "I appreciate you"? Do we remember the small gestures of helping each other, surprising one another, laughing together, going for walks together? Unfortunately, in the busyness of life, the small things are often forgotten. While intellectually we understand these oversights, emotionally the absence of these gestures may leave us feeling isolated or lonely. Rewriting family stories means paying attention to the small things.

In order to know a truth that is new to us, we need to experience the truth. This often requires behavioral change. Without changing behavior and directly experiencing the truth, our relationship with the truth may remain intellectual and not an experiential knowing. Moving forward in obedience to the truth expressed by God is not always easy and may involve some risk to the security, albeit misguided, provided by old patterns of behavior. This relationship is expressed well by Jesus in John 8:31-32. He offers the assurance that "the truth shall make you free." Practically, experiencing the truth often means that we must first act as if the old, irrational beliefs are not true and the new narrative is true.

Rewriting family stories takes time, patience, and often difficult emotional work. The benefits can be tremendous. Numerous resources are available to help in the practical aspects of dealing with emotional pain. Some may find that a qualified counselor can offer needed encouragement and support as they deal with painful messages. Regardless of how and when we begin the process, we can know with certainty "that Christ may dwell in [our] hearts by faith; that [we], being rooted and grounded in love, may be able to comprehend with all saints what is the breadth, and length, and depth, and height; and to know the love of Christ, which passeth knowledge, that [we] might be filled with all the fulness of God. Now unto him that is able to do exceeding abundantly above all that we ask or think, according to the power that worketh in us, unto him be glory in the church by Christ Jesus throughout all ages, world without end. Amen" (Eph. 3:17-21).

CHAPTER 7

Examining Messages from Our Families

Asa R. Sphar and Kristyn Carver

Few things are more precious and untainted than a mother holding her newborn baby. This is a picture of innocence, a new baby who has not yet experienced the sting of betrayal or the pain of rejection. This new life has no reason to be skeptical of the one who holds her or of the world that waits to be explored around her. Unfortunately, the difficulties of life lie crouching in the distance. As this little one grows, she will encounter events that will challenge her sense of security and tax her ability to trust so willingly. Those who surround her and the environment in which she develops will largely determine the impact upon her of such events. Her family and environment will either reinforce her belief that it is safe to trust and affirm her sense of worth or prove otherwise by promoting a sense of mistrust and shame.

Family researchers have suggested for nearly half a century that the element of trust is developed early in one's life. Erik Erikson proposed that trust versus mistrust is the first of eight psychological stages a person passes through during the human life cycle. In order for one to pass successfully to the next stage, this crisis must be faced and resolved. Should a person fail to leave this stage with a propensity to trust others, he would be forever limited in his ability to achieve healthy levels of emotional, relational, and spiritual adjustment. Even subsequent stages of development would be placed in jeopardy.

People learn either to trust or to mistrust based largely on the messages they receive from their families. Families that communicate affirmation and provide consistent, predictable, and reliable environments lay a foundation upon which healthy levels of trust can be established. In contrast, families that fail in these critical areas instill unhealthy levels of mistrust in their children. Unpredictable environments and unreliable, inconsistent, and/or abusive caregivers lead to the development of children who will have difficulty forming appropriate levels of need-satisfying attachments with others. If left unchallenged, strategies of avoidance and self-preservation developed during childhood will promote further emotional injury in adulthood when mistrust and suspicion lead to unnecessary alienation and disconnection from God, self, and others.

Second only to a person's need to develop healthy levels of trust is the individual's need to establish a sense of personal value or worth. Often confused with concepts such as self-esteem, this idea goes beyond just the need at times to feel positive or good about oneself. In fact, persons should not always feel positive about themselves or their behavior since healthy levels of appropriate guilt will emerge following sinful behavior. However, it is possible to feel guilty about one's own behavior and yet experience oneself as being a person of great worth or value. This distinction is critical. If children are to develop healthy identities with a powerful sense of their value and worth before God, they must experience this sense of valuing from their families while growing up. Hence, parents who consistently communicate messages of affirmation and acceptance toward their children are instilling in their children a critical sense of value and worth.

Conversely, parents who consistently communicate messages of shame and inadequacy will lead children to see themselves in faulty and damaging ways. What is shame? While books have been written on the subject, it is essentially experiencing oneself as being damaged, flawed, defective, or inherently unacceptable to others. While healthy forms of shame exist, often called discretionary shame, toxic shame is communicated both verbally and nonverbally in interpersonal communications between people. Through both deliberate and inadvertent words, facial expressions, body language, or vocal tones, shame is promoted when children experience themselves as being unacceptable, damaged, flawed, or unworthy of a parent's time and affection. The end result is that children who experience these messages face greater challenges in their quest to relate in a healthy and meaningful way to God, self, and others. By seeing themselves as flawed or deficient, they begin compensating for their perceived inadequacies in a variety of damaging ways. These strategies often undermine the formation and/or development of satisfying relationships with others.

While psychologists might trace the origin of trust and mistrust or self-worth and shame back to one's family, theologians likely would trace it back farther to the Garden of Eden. In the Book of Genesis, a picture of harmony surpassing that of a Norman Rockwell print is painted. Adam and Eve, God's precious creation, bask in the splendor of the paradise that surrounds them. They live at peace with God, self, and one another. All is well until Satan, in the form of the serpent, enters the stage and offers a seed of doubt. Through both direct questioning and subtle innuendo, Satan invites the couple to question the trustworthiness of God as well as the goodness of their own created state. Satan asks, "Yea, hath God said, Ye shall not eat of every tree of the garden? . . . Ye shall not surely die: for God doth know that in the day ye eat thereof, then your eyes shall be opened, and ye shall be as gods, knowing good and evil" (Gen. 3:1, 4-5).

Until this point, the couple has been content with their standing with God and in His trustworthiness as their Creator. They now fall prey to the temptation to question these assumptions by choosing to doubt the goodness of their human condition and the trustworthiness of their divine Creator. For the first time they experience mistrust, which will be followed by shame. Like the sins of the fathers being visited to the third and fourth generations,[1] the legacy of the Fall is that the sins of this original couple have continued to damage the nature and quality of relationships through the present day. We now see that Satan has compromised the very resources necessary to establish and maintain need-satisfying relationships with God, self, and others.

What is the answer to this age-old dilemma? The most obvious solution from a parenting perspective would be to raise children in a loving environment in which trust and self-worth are fostered—a home with parents who model trusting relationships and who send messages to their children that it is safe to be vulnerable and unashamed. Such homes operate in an atmosphere of support and affirmation, encouraging children to be confident and self-assured as they encounter each day. Unfortunately, far too many individuals are deprived of unconditional love, growing up in homes that are cold, critical, and chaotic—homes in which messages of shame are communicated and suspicion is always present. In this environment children learn to mistrust others and to fear true intimacy lest the shame of their personal inadequacy be exposed. So the question is, How might a person overcome these obstacles that have created barriers in his or her interpersonal relationships? This transformation is accomplished through intentional efforts directed at reconciling oneself to God, self, and others. As relationships in these three areas are repaired, one will begin to experience the joy of life and love as God intended.

In its simplest terms, to reconcile means to change or exchange. In the case of a mistrustful attitude, one would seek to change or exchange this attitude for another. It requires intentional effort to let go of feelings of mistrust that have been deeply ingrained and to challenge the messages of shame and inadequacy. When a person believes he is deficient as a human being, the sense of shame can be so overwhelming that reconciliation seems impossible. Though it may seem overwhelming, such a process was initiated through the atoning sacrifice of our Lord Jesus Christ, who, by dying and rising again as our Savior, communicated once and for all the trustworthiness of our Creator and the worth of His creation. By virtue of His atoning work, we now hold the possibility of finding reconciliation and healing even from a lifetime of hurt and sadness caused by shame and mistrust.

In order to appropriate fully the resources found at the cross, we should consider carefully the nature of both trust and an individual's worth before God. To trust means to choose to place confidence in the positive intentions and truthfulness of the object of that confidence. Trust can be cultivated over time but never fully earned. In that sense, trust is a gift of consciously choosing to invest support in the object of our trust. Given the inherent fallibility of human beings and our limited capacity to know another's intentions completely, an element of risk is always involved in the act of trusting. In fact, in a fallen world, wisdom dictates that we must preserve the right to be mistrusting of certain people and/or situations. However, excessive mistrust compromises our judgment and inhibits the development of healthy relationships with God, self, and others. Therefore we need to embrace the inherent risks involved in pursuing meaningful connection by working to establish healthy levels of trust. This choice will enable us to renew and invigorate existing relationships and form new, more satisfying relationships with others. Coupled with a need to foster trust in our circle of relationships is our need to work to understand and assimilate the knowledge of our inherent worth to our Maker. Persons who have been compromised by a history of shame and mistrust can accomplish this sense of worth by embarking on a threefold strategy of reconciliation with God, self, and others.

Reconciliation with God

The Fall has left humankind with distorted messages and emotions that often hinder individuals from trusting God and looking to Him for direction. Feelings of being unacceptable and unlovable also have led to alienation from God, often resulting in attempts to seek self-deliverance through the pursuit of knowledge, money, sex, power, science, youth, or anything but God.

Freedom from the bondage of human striving is possible only when one chooses to embrace, through faith, the grace of unconditional acceptance found in the Cross. God's willingness to allow Christ to die for us and to bear our shame demonstrated the trustworthiness of God and the value of His creation. To accept the love of God through the gift of His Son is to liberate us from the enslavement of damaging messages and emotions and to free us to embrace a new relationship with God. Ironically, what was desperately grasped at in the Fall has been given lovingly through the Cross.

Reconciliation with Others

Anyone who has grown up in a home in which criticism was frequent, acceptance was not offered, and violations of trust were common knows how difficult it can be to move beyond this past to embrace others. Years of scars can create a callus designed to protect tender wounds from further pain. The result of these calluses is often shame and an inability to trust. In the Gospel of John, Jesus told His followers to "love one another."[2] Loving others is difficult when relationships are tainted by mistrust. The ability to overcome these obstacles is found only in Christ. When individuals live by the Spirit, they will be enabled to love their neighbors, to bless others rather than curse them, and to empower others rather than dominate them. When spiritual filling occurs, the reciprocal love of God will flow in relationships and allow freedom for people to experience the mutual need satisfaction that was intended to characterize the nature of relationships from the beginning.

Just as shame is born in the context of failed relationships, its remedy is likewise found in the context of restored relationships—relationships that communicate the love of unconditional acceptance and grace that individuals so desperately need. Perfect acceptance awaits those who claim their right relationship with God. It is through God's creation that perfect acceptance finds its most similar and fundamental expression. We who follow Jesus serve vicariously as His hands and feet, one body in Christ seeking to minister grace to the walking wounded in our midst. Christians have the opportunity to be the instruments that God uses to touch those who are broken and consumed by feelings of inadequacy. The ability to move beyond injuries from the past and to form satisfying, mutually trustworthy relationships depends on the corrective trust-engendering experiences discovered in healthy relationships with others. God calls His children to be conduits of the acceptance and trustworthiness they personally have experienced as a result of His grace.

Reconciliation with Self

Since the great deception in the Garden of Eden, humans have wrestled with the temptation to devalue themselves. Children who grow up without much-needed affirmation and unconditional love often doubt their worth and feel ashamed of who they are. Likewise, adolescents who measure themselves against the standards of media and models also feel inferior. Hurtful relationships, unmet expectations, broken confidences, and betrayed commitments all call into question one's worth. Individuals rely on other fallen creatures to help determine their personal value. Improper comparisons, such as the one made in the Garden, result in self-loathing and shame. Ultimately, a person's sense of value or worth can be realized fully only when he comes to recognize the depth of his sin and the liberation and restoration he has been granted through the grace of Jesus Christ. One's value as God's creation is manifested most clearly in the value of the atoning sacrifice of His Son. Jesus' death on the behalf of humankind reveals and demonstrates once and for all how much God loves and values His children. His sacrifice also forever contradicts the shameful message perpetuated by Satan that God's supreme creation, humanity, whom He proclaimed to be "very good," should be held in disrepute. Therefore, people must learn to change the damaging messages that give rise to shame and mistrust in order to prevent the cycle of distorted emotions from infecting their relationships with others. Messages of personal unacceptability must be confronted, and the message that God's children are truly new creatures in Christ must be embraced.[3]

Summary

Families play a critical role in modeling a pattern of relating to their children that will either be characterized by trust or mistrust, affirmation or shame. In order to raise children to be more trusting than mistrusting and more affirming than shaming, parents consistently must demonstrate these attitudes on a personal level. When couples cultivate a relationship that is characterized by trust and affirmation, they can leave a profound legacy for their children and the children's future relationships. Additionally, by offering genuine praise and affirmation for specific qualities and behaviors demonstrated by their children, parents can reinforce their children's sense of value and worth. When parents identify for their children the qualities and talents they see in them, they will reinforce their children's sense of uniqueness and value.

When an individual fails to develop a healthy sense of self in the family of origin, that person often experiences difficulty with interpersonal relationships. It is important that adults not remain stuck in the mistrusting, shame-based messages from the past. In order to move forward, one must reconcile with God, self, and others by identifying and challenging these distorted messages. By accepting and embracing the love that God offers, one can begin truly to heal from the wounds of the past and learn to love and trust again.

CHAPTER 8

Receiving the Blessing

Argile Smith

Every morning, ministers across the country get out of their beds and into their work in the corners of the Kingdom where God has placed them. What motivates them to go about their work with passion? What prompts them to strive toward excellence in ministry day after day? Some ministers are passionate about their work because they have a profound sense of fulfillment. God called them to ministry, and they have found serving Him to be the most fulfilling thing they could ever do with their lives.

Other ministers, however, go about their day in search of something. Even though they are Christians who have surrendered to God's call to ministry, they still have an empty place in their hearts, and so far their work has not filled it. But they keep at it, hoping that somehow their work will eventually give them the fulfillment they crave.

The difference between the two categories of ministers becomes most obvious at the end of the day. At night, when all the meetings of the day have been attended, the phone calls returned, the emergencies addressed, and the worship services prepared, some ministers thank God again for the chance to do something they love so much. Others, however, beg God again for a way out. Or they beat themselves over their heads for what they didn't get to finish in the daylight hours. Or they numb the ache of feeling so alone by watching television late into the night until they can drift off into a troubled sleep.

What's wrong with such empty-hearted ministers? Has God really called them to ministry? Do they need to love God more? Have they failed to live out the disciplines of the faith properly? Are they hiding some secret sin?

Maybe. But, then again, maybe not.

Indeed, their problem may stem from a number of issues ranging from an authentic call to ministry to a personal walk with God. On the other hand, their problem could be related to something else entirely, to a phenomenon that's been around a long time. An age-old phenomenon, it's something that's brought up again and again in the Bible. For the last couple of decades, it has been the subject of some significant work by counselors like Myron Madden.[1] Thankfully, it's a recurring subject of ongoing conversation between ministers, seminary students, and faculty as well as other helping professionals.

It's something that's often referred to as a blessing. Having a blessing helps us to live as a whole person. Lacking it can leave us with a relational hole in our heart. Perhaps it's what's missing in the lives of many miserable ministers.

The blessing gets at one of the most crucial themes intrinsic in the Great Commandment,[2] the core Bible passage that underscores the imperative for ministers to develop healthy interpersonal relationship skills. Stated as the divine imperative to love God, love others, and love ourselves, the Great Commandment forms the basis of everything we do as we minister in the name of Jesus Christ. Accordingly, it serves as the foundation for the relationships we nurture as we carry out the Great Commission.[3]

The balance between loving God, others, and ourselves has to be considered if we intend to go the distance in ministry and find fulfillment in it. Loving God nurtures our love for others and vice versa. Somewhere in the process God intends for us to grow in our love for ourselves. Of course, this imperative does not give us permission to be self-indulgent. Quite the contrary, it implies something more penetrating and permanent. Simply stated, God wants us to accept ourselves. Just think about what could happen if we truly accepted ourselves as unique people created and redeemed by Jesus Christ to be God's children.

The reality of the blessing belongs in the center of this discussion of self-acceptance. Like other realities of our lives worth discussing, the salient features of the blessing can be found in the Bible. In particular, the blessing stands out as a major theme in two prominent passages: Genesis 49 and Mark 10. Studying the development of this vital theme in these passages will provide a context for you to ask yourself whether you have appropriated the blessing of Jesus in your life and ministry.

Genesis 49: Jacob and His Sons

Jacob certainly seemed to have an appreciation of the value of a blessing, and so did his mother, Rebekah. According to Genesis 27, she hatched a plot in which Jacob would steal the blessing rightfully due his minutes-older twin brother, Esau. Jacob seemed to be a more than willing participant in the plot, following his mother's instruction to swipe the blessing from his father, Isaac, who was old and blind and an easy target for a deceiver. By the time Esau found out about what Jacob had done, it was too late. Isaac had already given Esau's blessing to Jacob.

So began Jacob's story. In the years ahead it would be full of twists and turns, some of them curious and at least one of them heartbreaking. Jacob must have regretted waking up the day he heard that a wild animal had killed Joseph, his favorite son. Years later, he learned that the news he heard was actually a lie concocted by jealous brothers who had sold Joseph into slavery. Then he found out that Joseph was still alive and well. Eventually he and his family moved to Egypt to be near Joseph.[4]

Some time later, when Jacob knew that he wouldn't live much longer, he called for his sons from his deathbed. Genesis 49 indicates that he had one purpose in mind for the gathering. He wanted to give each of his twelve sons a blessing. There, gathered around their old father, twelve men, now grown and with families of their own, listened as Jacob called each one of them by name and uttered what he considered to be an appropriate blessing for each one of them. It must have been a solemn moment as they heard their father give them a glimpse of their destinies, telling them what would become of them in due time.

Cultures change across the centuries. A blessing like the one Jacob gave to each of his sons in ancient Egypt doesn't carry the same cultural weight in twenty-first-century America. Even so, two realities have spanned the vast differences in centuries and cultures: parents still can give their children a forecast of the kinds of people they will become, and children still crave a blessing from their parents.

In our day, a parental blessing may not be uttered in a deathbed scene. In fact, it might not even be one single, solitary utterance at all. Instead, a parental blessing may be something that a child accumulates across the years that he or she lives at home with a parent, parents, grandparents, or any other authority figures in the family.

Children who have received a parental blessing know for certain that their parents love them no matter what. With that affirmation of love comes the assurance that their parents believe in them. It's a forgone conclusion for them that their parents think they will be important people who will make a difference in whatever they do. Such fortunate children tend to grow up and live out a deeply embedded message of approval. As a result, their self-concept has been shaped in large measure by the blessing from proud and wise parents.

Other children are not so fortunate. They didn't get a blessing from their parents, so they don't enjoy a sense of approval. Instead, they received another message, one that has troubled many of them even through their journey into adulthood. Even when God calls them to ministry and they surrender to Him without reservation, the absence of approval from their parents may still trouble them. It can haunt them or leave them with an aching sense that something is still missing. In turn, they may shape their days and nights around doing things in search of a blessing.

Unlike those fortunate ministers who live with a sense of approval, ministers in search of a blessing live with the gnawing notion that they don't measure up. It's something that eats at them constantly, and no matter what they do to try to measure up, it just won't go away. They can accomplish almost impossible feats, but it doesn't satisfy them. They can earn advanced seminary degrees, but they still feel empty and lonely on graduation day. Or they can work tirelessly to lead their churches to do some remarkable things, but they don't enjoy the affirmation that accompanies all the awards from denominational leaders. They can portray to their congregations a kind of chummy closeness in their families, but in reality they can't remember the last time they laughed with their spouse or children at the dinner table. Worst of all, they wear a smile as they move through their day, but inside they wish they could run away and never come back.

Measuring up can be impossible if someone with parental authority in your life has told you that you never will. Even with all the signs of success around them to show otherwise, people in search of a blessing can only allow themselves to believe that they will continue to fall short. Likewise, they have trouble convincing themselves that they are actually responsible for the successes that may come their way. Because they don't think they are good enough, it's almost impossible for them to say that they deserve anything good.

So far, the notion of a parental blessing contoured by the picture provided in Genesis 49 raises two questions. First, if you didn't receive a parental blessing, what can you do about it? Second, if you did receive a blessing from your parents, what's next for you?

Mark 10: Jesus and the Children

To answer the two questions, Mark's account of Jesus with the children may be helpful. Like the story of Jacob, this story provides a picturesque context in which the issues can be explored further and some answers can be suggested. But unlike Jacob's story in which grown sons came to a dying father for a blessing, Mark's story involves young children being brought to Jesus so He would touch them.[5] So does Luke's version of the story, although he identifies the children as infants.[6]

Matthew adds a bit of detail to the story when he writes that the little children had been brought to Jesus so He could put his hands on them and pray.[7]

Jesus had an extremely high regard for the children who had been waiting for Him by the roadside. That's obvious by the way He stopped His journey long enough to tend to them. The road He traveled took Him from Capernaum to Jerusalem where He would face the Cross. Although nothing else would distract Him from getting to His destination, little children on the roadside could make Him stop for a while.

His indignation toward the disciples who were hindering the children from coming to Him also showed His high regard for the children. Perhaps the disciples thought the children were blocking the road or making too much noise when they issued their stern rebuke to them. Regardless of their reason for doing it, Jesus became angry with the disciples for speaking harshly to the children.

More important, Jesus' value of children was obvious in the way He used them to personify the character traits of the citizenry of the Kingdom of God. On His way to the Cross, He needed to leave a lasting imprint in the disciples' minds as to what a Kingdom citizen should look like. So He showed them a child.

His imprint lasted a lifetime for John, one of the twelve disciples who walked with Jesus on the road. John was an old man by the time he wrote his letters to the churches. In his first epistle, he referred to his fellow Christians as little children.[8] Apparently Jesus had taught John well when He stopped along the road to the Cross to bless the children.

Paul also used the same picture word to describe Christians.[9] Granted, Paul didn't know Jesus until some time after His death and resurrection. On the road to Damascus, however, Jesus changed his life forever.[10] As a result, Paul brought up children as a picture word to describe who we are in the Lord.

Just for a moment, ponder for yourself what Jesus said. A person redeemed by Christ is a child of God, and so is a believer who has surrendered his or her life to be a minister. A

Christian as God's child is a compelling metaphor that allows us to see ourselves in an intimate relationship with our Father. In that relationship we couple our naiveté with His wisdom, our helplessness with His strength, our trust with His integrity, and our vulnerability with His protection. Most of all, we couple our need for a blessing with His eagerness to bless us.

As you study what Jesus did on the road with the children, pay close attention to His presence, His touch, and His voice. He could have been anywhere He wanted at that moment, so He obviously wanted to be with the children who were waiting for Him. By stopping there to be with them, He affirmed how much they mattered to Him. His presence with them spoke volumes about the way He valued them.

His touch affirmed the children as well. His hands already had touched people throughout Palestine, making them well, restoring their sight, removing their handicaps, and even bringing them back to life. Now His hands touched the children, giving them a blessing. With His hands resting on them, they knew He considered them to be important.

The children felt His gentle hands resting on them, and they heard His voice as He prayed for them. Like His hands, His voice had been responsible for some God-sized miracles. He spoke to storms and they disappeared, to demons and they ran for cover, to religious rule-keepers and they were silenced. We don't know exactly what Jesus said to the children. But we can rest assured that He spoke to them and to the Father on their behalf in a way that showed how much He cared about them. It's another in the long list of God-sized miracles Jesus performed with His voice.

Do you remember when you received Jesus Christ as your personal Savior and Lord? Think back to that experience and recall His presence, His touch, and His voice. He came to you when you were eternally lost. Under conviction in His presence, you confessed your sin and surrendered your life to Him. In a way He touched you at that moment, resting His hands of approval on you. As He spoke from His heart to yours, you heard His voice, and you knew He had forgiven you and made you His child.

The day He saved you was the day He blessed you. When you received Him like a child, He gave you the most important blessing you will ever receive. If you can appropriate it in your life, it will make a world of difference in the way you minister in His name.

Now it's time to answer the two questions that were raised earlier. First, what if you didn't receive a blessing from your parents? You could spend your life trying to earn one, but your efforts would be futile. Or you can ask the Lord to help you appropriate the blessing He has already given you when He saved you. If you do, He can put a spring in your step as you serve Him out of a heart grateful for blessing you. In due time you may find yourself using Paul's words to thank God "who hath blessed us with all spiritual blessings in heavenly places in Christ" (Eph. 1:3).

Second, if you did receive a blessing from your parents, don't discount the superlative way Jesus blessed you when He came into your life. The core issue in discipleship is maturing in Christ so we can reflect His character in our thoughts, words, values, beliefs, and actions. Growing in Him means we acknowledge what He has done for us as the greatest gift we have ever received. Our parents can bless us in a number of ways, and we honor them for what they have done. But a parental blessing can't address the eternal issues that all of us have to face. Only Jesus can do something about our eternity, our sin debt, our need to be forgiven, and our need for an intimate relationship with God.

The more we grasp the eternal impact of what Jesus did for us, the more we will celebrate the way He alone blessed us when He saved us. When we appropriate His superlative blessing in our lives, we can learn to minister to others in His name out of a grateful heart. In Him we have found our fulfillment. Sensing the whisper of His voice, the touch of His hand, and the awareness of His presence, we know how blessed we are to be God's children.

What gets you out of bed in the morning? What's on your mind when you come to the end of the day? Hopefully, the answer to both questions points you toward the same answer: Jesus has blessed you. Are you living out the blessing He gave you?

CHAPTER 9

Getting Dad's Approval:
A Testimony

Argile Smith

If I had to choose just one word to describe my dad, it would have to be *murky*. For most all of my life he seemed to be living just below an overcast sky, dreary but not completely gloomy. It's as if sadness simmered in his soul.

He had good reason to be that way. Born in 1906 on a farm in deep south Mississippi, he was one of twelve children. When he was eleven, his father sent him to work on the farm of a relative. He married a beautiful young woman when he was nineteen, and for twelve years they enjoyed a happy life. In fact, word has it that he and she looked like little children playing and laughing together. One time I saw a photograph of him and her leaning against the hood of a Model A (or T, I am not really sure about the difference between them) and sitting on the bumper. He had his arms wrapped around her, and both of them smiled like young lovers. Indeed, they looked happy.

Together they had four children, all of them healthy and smart. My dad's family seemed destined for good things.

Then his wife died all too suddenly. Her spleen had ruptured, and emergency surgery couldn't save her. In a picture of her that someone showed me years later, taken when her body was lying in her coffin, she was still so very pretty. But four children had lost their mother, and my dad had lost the love of his life. And that was not pretty at all. In fact, it must have been one of the ugliest moments of his life.

They say that when my dad's wife died, a part of him died

too. They must have been right, and what I saw in his murky countenance must have been the corpse of a buried relationship with someone he must have really loved.

For the next couple of years, he wandered along from day to day, taking care of his children and his sanity the best way he could. Then he married again, this time to someone almost twenty years younger. In fact, she was only a couple of years older than his oldest daughter.

He and his young wife set out to make a future together, but they had trouble at the start. Their first child was born with cerebral palsy. It crippled him to the point that he couldn't walk or talk in a way that most folks could understand. Neither could he feed himself, change his own clothes, or go the bathroom by himself. Bound to a wheelchair and a bed, he required constant attention from his parents.

And that's exactly what they gave him. I never recall them getting frustrated or angry with their very special child. Quite the contrary, they always treated him with respect and dignity, and in the process they showed how much they loved him. As far as they were concerned, love never failed. I didn't learn that Bible truth by reading 1 Corinthians 13. I learned it by watching my dad and mom take care of my brother. Together they gave all of their children an excellent example of how far you will go for people when you love them.

My dad and mom had eight more children. That's right, four plus nine equals thirteen. I have six brothers and six sisters. I am number eleven in the line of thirteen. They also had a herd of dairy cows, along with pigs, chickens, and a few yard dogs.

Five of the oldest children had left home by the time I came along. I remember eight of us children living there. And all the cows, pigs, and chickens were there, and the dogs stayed around too. Every day my dad and mom had to shoulder the load of making sure that all of those hungry mouths were fed. For my dad, it meant getting up every morning of his life at 4:00 A.M. so he could get to the dairy barn to begin the chore of milking the cows. For my mom, it meant getting up every day of her life at the same time and going through a regimented routine of her own. Her morning included getting children out of bed and out the door to do their chores and back inside to eat breakfast so they could get ready for school before the bus came for them at 7 A.M. Then she would go to the barn and take over so my dad could go to work.

My dad built houses, and he could do everything that was involved with turning wood, brick, concrete, and wire into a home. He was particularly good at building chimneys, and he had plenty of finished products in the community to demonstrate his master craftsmanship.

He was an excellent farmer. Every year he planted and harvested most of the food necessary for all the hungry mouths under his care. Thanks to him and my mother, we always had plenty to eat.

Milking cows, building houses, and working his farm, however, took their toll on him. He lived tired. He went to bed tired, and he woke up tired. Looking back, I cannot imagine how bone-tired he must have been most of the time I was living at home.

But he never said much about it. Fact is, he never said much about anything. Most of his story came to me by way of relatives or family friends. He never told me his story, so I was left on my own to try to figure out why he seemed so sad, so grumpy, so distant, so murky. I figured that it must have been because he didn't like me.

They say that children are wonderful observers, but poor interpreters. I would be a good case study for that aphorism. I observed every detail I could about my dad, but I missed it altogether when it came to the interpreting part. In my defense, I was only a child then, and I didn't know any better. Most kids still don't know any better. The sad thing is that those same kids grow up to be adults who carry around a small mountain of unnecessary pain due to the way they misread what they saw growing up.

My dad was about fifty years old when I was born. Do the math, and you can understand how the wide generation gap got even wider by the time I became a teenager. When I was fifteen, he was around sixty-five. When he was fifteen, the year was around 1920. When I was fifteen, it was about 1970. His silence about what happened to him through those fifty years, and my conclusion that he didn't like me, made for a relationship filled with harmful ambiguities.

My family believed in God, but we didn't go to church. Dairy cows didn't take a sabbath rest, and my brother in a wheelchair didn't need the stress of being in crowds of people. Also, my dad didn't talk about his spirituality very much. You could see it, however, in the way he behaved. For instance, during planting season he would always leave the garden after all the seeds had been sowed into the rows of dirt and say the same thing: "Now it's up to the Master."

Much later, years in fact, I talked to my dad about his relationship with God. He told me about becoming a Christian when he was twelve years old. Talking about it with a certain confidence, he was sure that something eternal happened to him the day he got saved.

Thanks to some of the folks like Roy and Marie Black at Juniper Grove Baptist Church, I heard about Jesus Christ. I had watched Billy Graham on television, so I knew a little about what Jesus had done for me. The Blacks took it from there. They came out, picked up us kids, and delivered us to Vacation Bible School. I guess you could say the experience "took" with me. Later, they made sure I had a way to church on Sunday. So did Robert Dunn, the next pastor of the church. Consequently, in August 1971, I received Christ as my Savior and Lord. In that same year, I surrendered to His call to preach.

I have often wondered what would have happened to me if the folks from the church hadn't come. What would have happened if Roy Black had not given me my first Bible and shown me the love of Jesus in the process? What if Marie Black hadn't loved me enough to teach me how to sing? What if Robert Dunn hadn't taken me down the Roman Road that hot August night after worship when I told him that I needed someone to show me how to be saved?

Somehow the two experiences of knowing Jesus personally and surrendering to His call hadn't gone deep enough into my soul to do anything about my stifled relationship with my dad. I didn't tell him about either of those wonderful experiences. Eventually he found out, but he never spoke about them. I took his silence as just one more reason for me to believe that he didn't like me.

By this time I had begun to make my list of reasons to be angry with my dad. And I added to it every time he didn't do something I wished he would do. Over the years the list got to be fairly long.

He didn't come to any of my school programs.

He didn't come to my high school graduation.

He didn't come to my college graduation.

He didn't come to either of my two seminary graduations.

He didn't say anything about my dissertation except, "When are you going to get a job?"

He didn't give me a dime toward my education.

He didn't attend my wedding.

He didn't come to church to hear me preach a sermon.

He didn't visit any of the churches in which I served as staff minister or pastor.

He didn't . . . As you can tell, I got to be pretty good at making my list.

There I was, a young preacher now married with small children in tow, trying to share the love of Christ with others in my church and my community. At the same time I was carrying around the pain of not being liked by my dad. I would have done anything to get his nod of approval, and I resented all the times I tried but to no avail.

You might say that in time I became two people. On the outside I was the hard-working pastor with a young family. On the inside, though, I was a lonely young man with an aching need for his dad's approval. As a result of the duplicity, I had an awfully unhealthy self-concept. Always on my guard, I became coy in my relationships with other people. And I gladly tried to erase who I really was in Christ in order to become the person I thought the people around me wanted me to be.

I had trusted Jesus with so many of my personal struggles, but not this one. Maybe I didn't think it would do any good. Perhaps I felt guilty for feeling so miserable, and I didn't want to make my situation worse by exposing my dark side to the light of Christ's presence.

But the Lord wouldn't leave me alone, even when I tried to keep Him at arm's length. He kept on nudging me to acknowledge the hard fact that I had to be the same person on the outside and the inside if I wanted to find any fulfillment at all in ministry.

One night I was in my study, and my wife and children were in bed asleep. I was reading a series of sermons from Romans 6:23. The sermons focused on the difference between the wages of sin and the gift of God. Much to my surprise, the passage gripped me, pushing me to remember the August night when I asked Christ to forgive me of my sins and come into my life. Then the rest of the truth hit me, something that I had shared with others countless times, but I had overlooked it for myself. I was a sinner, but Jesus loved me enough to give me eternal life.

For the very first time, I understood something new about my struggle with my dad. I am sure the Lord had tried to show it to me earlier, but I wouldn't see it. Now I could.

If my dad would show me that he loved me, that would be a good thing. It would soothe the ache in my heart. But when the Lord showed me how much He loved me by giving me eternal life, that was the best thing. His gift had already filled up the empty place in my heart when He saved me. Because of the love of Jesus, I could give up the struggle for my dad's love.

Somehow that fresh awareness of God's gift began to soften my hardening heart, and I began to cry. I think I wept most of the night. The next day found me broken and hungry to know my Lord better. I read one Bible book after another, this time not for sermons, but for me. And I couldn't keep from crying, especially when I heard the people in my congregation sing about His "amazing grace . . . that saved a wretch like me."[1]

Even as I think about it now, I still get a lump in my throat.

My Jesus loved me enough to give me life in Him. I can't fathom any other demonstration of love that comes close to it. The night He saved me was the day He blessed me. I can't figure out why He did it, but I am forever in His debt for doing it.

Through the experience, Jesus settled me, helping me to be comfortable in my own skin. He also enabled me to get His perspective on the ministry to which He has called me, and He showed me how I could find joy in Kingdom work. Most of all, He gave me His peace.

And He helped me love my dad no matter what. For the first time, I didn't need anything from my dad. I didn't need to carry around the pain of my struggle with him any more. I could let it go. I could tear up my list.

My story about my relationship with my dad has a very happy ending. A few years later he got really sick. The flu strain that infected him was potent, and it almost killed him. While he was trying to fight off the flu virus, he must have been wrestling with the Lord at the same time. He never talked about it, but I could see it by the way he behaved after he got well. At Christmas, for example, he did something he had never done before. He wrote a note to my mom, put it in an envelope with her name on the outside, and laid it on one of the branches of the Christmas tree. In the envelope with the note he had put some money. On the note he had scribbled, "Just because I love you."

He also began to talk a little more openly about his relationship with God, although still not too much. He told me more of the story about how he was led to Christ when he was twelve years old: A pastor invited all the boys and girls in the community to his house to play. He played with them, invited them to have lunch with him, and taught them Bible verses. He led my dad to Christ and baptized him in a creek. My dad told the story with a twinkle in his eye, as if he still remembered the fun and games and the love of Jesus around the pastor's table.

There's one more thing he did that I will never forget. Not long before he died, he asked me for some tapes of my sermons. Of course, I was more than willing to comply with his request. My mom reported to me that he listened to them all the time. When his friends came to visit him, he liked to play one of the tapes for them. He always told them that he thought I was a good preacher.

That's right. My story has a happy ending, thanks to my Savior.

PART III

Your Relationships in Your Home

CHAPTER 10

Sharing the Joys and Sorrows in Ministry

Argile and Connie Smith

Working with people in a ministry setting has its ups and downs. Knowing about them can help you be better prepared to deal with them together when they come your way. And you can rest assured that they will come your way, and from directions you never thought possible.

The sorrows related to working with people in the church will break your heart, but the joys will be a source of deep and abiding fulfillment. The heartbreakers of ministry come in the shape of problems, but the joys always come wrapped in the package called people. Dealing with people in the church and the problems that come with them requires you to strike a balance in your home. You and your family have to find a way to account for the heartbreakers as well as the joy makers in your relationships with the people in the place where God has called you to minister.

The Heartbreakers

As you work with people in your church, keep in mind that problems can come from anywhere. They can take many shapes, but some of the most common problems have to do with unrealistic expectations, almost constant visibility, nearly impossible schedules, and costly mistakes. Each of these problems can have an impact on your home.

By the way, keep in mind that in this article you will come

across some stories about actual situations. The names of the people involved, however, have been changed.

Unrealistic Expectations

Folks in the church can nurture some fairly steep expectations of their minister. For instance, you may be called to be the pastor of a church that has experienced a succession of short-term relationships with previous pastors. In such a revolving-door setting, the people in the church generally tend to collect all of the attributes they liked about the previous pastors, mold them together, and expect you to live out each one of them yourself.

The only way you can overcome the situation is to stay long enough at the church to break the mold. Until it's broken, you have to live with the endless criticisms that may come your way in the meantime. And sometimes the meantime can seem like a lifetime.

Rick didn't have the problem of following a series of short-term ministers when he accepted the call to serve on the staff of a growing church, but he had to deal with an equally troubling problem. The previous minister had served the congregation well, and he had been faithful to the church for a long time. Everyone loved him, and they had a tough time letting go of him, even though he had moved to a ministry setting far, far away.

When Rick began his ministry, he and his wife, Becky, noticed that the welcoming smiles on the faces of the church people only barely shrouded another emotion. Rick began to get the distinct impression that they resented him for being there. He didn't understand why they would feel that way. Rick had been approached by the search committee, not the other way around. The staff ministry position had been vacant for some time before the committee began to talk with him. He hadn't pushed his way into the staff position. Quite the contrary, the position had been offered to him. Why would these people resent his being there? Every day he took that question home with him, and he and Becky struggled in search of an answer.

Over time, Rick observed that the subtle shades of resentment gave way to more straightforward messages that he was not being well received by the people. Complaints about his performance had been directed to both him and his pastor. With a track record of dedicated and capable ministry, Rick grew frustrated with the complaints and the unrealistic expectations placed on him.

Ready to resign and move on, Rick talked to his pastor about his frustrations. After he shared his sorrow and disappointment over the poor reception he had received, his pastor offered Rick another perspective on the situation. The people in the church resented Rick, the pastor contended, simply because he wasn't the previous minister. They still had sorrow in their hearts because a minister they loved so much was no longer there. They couldn't let him go, much less put their arm around the minister who had come to take his place.

Seeing the situation from that perspective, Rick could begin to look past the cold reception he had gotten. He and Becky asked God to enable them to be patient as they waited for the people to accept Rick. God answered their prayers. Time took care of unrealistic expectations placed on Rick, and he and Becky enjoyed a long, effective ministry in the church.

Almost Constant Visibility

Being a minister makes you a very public person. You and your family become highly visible and, therefore, vulnerable to the scrutiny of church members as well as everyone else in the community.

Living in such a fish bowl puts a minister's family on display. The high-profile pedestal provides a front-row seat for people to see the good, the bad, and the ugly in a minister's home. Having the spotlight on you and the people you love can create a stressful situation that can become unbearable, especially if someone decides to shine the spotlight on you in a way that's cruel.

Danny and Stephanie knew that the church they served had a troubled past. Tension and strife had characterized the congregation for years, but Danny and Stephanie also knew that

God had called them there. Every day they prayed for things to change.

Just as Danny sensed that his congregation was turning a corner toward better relationships, he got a letter in the mail. The envelope didn't have a return address, the letter didn't have a signature, and the writer didn't have a heart. As Danny read it, he couldn't believe the cruelty that had been scratched on paper. The anonymous writer had accused him of being a poor preacher and Stephanie of being a pitiful pastor's wife who allowed their two preschoolers to look like they had been dressed in a salvage store.

The letter crushed Danny and Stephanie. Instinctively they wanted to close their curtains and withdraw from their congregation. They realized that someone in the church had been watching them and waiting. At just the right time, the nameless writer threw a literary rock and shattered their ministerial fish bowl.

They never found out who wrote the letter. But neither did they ever reveal to anyone that they had received it. After that experience, however, they never opened letters that didn't have a return address. And they asked the Lord to give them His strength as they worked through the heartbreaks that came along with living in the spotlight of their congregation.

Nearly Impossible Schedules

People's needs don't take a day off. For that reason, a minister can't either. You may be able to take a day away from the office, a day away for the sake of your mental, emotional, or spiritual health. But you can never really consider yourself "off the clock." By necessity, you have to maintain vigilance even when you try to relax.

Some ministers don't take the 24-7 set-up seriously enough. As a result they fail to develop the needed skill of negotiating the ebb and flow of stress in ministry. When they can rest, they work instead. Then, when they need the reserves to work harder, they have little or nothing to give. The heartbreaking spiral of burnout begins before they know it.

Others suffer in the process too. Ignoring the opportunities to shut down and regroup can have a painful effect on your family. Your spouse can get the impression that the only way to get your attention is to call the church office and ask for an appointment to see you. Your children can grow bitter at the reality that the church has stolen you from them. They can resent the phone ringing at all hours of the day or night, robbing them of your attention. And they can even get frustrated with the few times you are home as they notice that while you are there, you are not really there. Your mind and heart are somewhere else, presumably at the church.

Granted, your people need you, but your spouse and children need you too. In addition, you need to give yourself some down time. But you have only twenty-four hours in a day, and you have only seven days in the week.

Andrea had to face the on-call dilemma when she became a staff minister at a church on the edge of her city. The ministry opportunity she accepted at the church was brand new to the congregation, so she had to build it from the ground up. Making it effective meant investing herself in it completely.

Therein lay the problem. Andrea's husband had been killed in an automobile accident, leaving her a widow. All by herself, she had to shoulder the load of caring for their son, Christopher, who was in the third grade at the time. He remembered when his dad died and lived in fear that his mom would be leaving him next. And even though Andrea's husband had been gone more than a year, she still missed him. It would be easy for her to immerse herself in her ministry to numb the pain of her own grief. But Christopher needed her, and so did her church.

As she worked through the problem, she noticed that she started to resent the people in the church for needing her so much. At the same time, she was beginning to lose her patience with Christopher. Something had to be done if she intended to go the distance in ministry without creating distance between herself and the people who needed her.

God showed her that the place to begin was her calendar. He brought to her attention that even though she thought she was managing her calendar, in reality it was actually managing her. When she searched for time to be with Christopher, she couldn't; all of her time slots had been given to people at the church.

That's when it dawned on her—or rather God opened her eyes to the fact—that she had to take control of her time, and not the other way around. She rearranged her calendar so she could be at home with Christopher on Thursday nights. She felt good about herself as she wrote "appointment" over the Thursday night blocks for every week. Then she wrote the same word over one afternoon each week that she had set aside just for herself.

Some time later, she got a call from the chairperson of an important committee to which she had been assigned. He wanted to set a meeting for—you guessed it—Thursday night. She held her breath for a second and then blurted out the words, "I have an appointment for that night." Feeling a little guilty about what she had said, she tried to explain, "I prom- ised Christopher that I would be with him that night."

Silently she waited for the sigh of disgust and the short lec- ture about priorities. But she didn't get either one. All she got was the reply, "All right, well what about Wednesday night before prayer meeting?"

"Yes, that time will be fine," she said, a little surprised at how easy it was to protect her time with her son once she reserved it. As she continued to plan her calendar along the lines of her priorities, she discovered that people generally tended to respect her schedule and work with it.

Costly Mistakes

Not all of the problems that accompany our relationships in the church start with the people. Some of them, if not most of them, we bring on ourselves. They result from not making the vital task of nurturing relationships with the folks in the con- gregation a high priority.

Forced terminations and church splits have dotted the ecclesiastical landscape for a long time now, and the situation doesn't seem to be getting much better. Sadly, many of them could have been avoided if ministers had worked on building bridges instead of walls. The following comments have been made by people in churches about ministers who are unwilling to work on relationships.

- Ministers are more comfortable on the Internet than they are in the intensive care unit.
- Ministers wish that all of us senior adults would just go away.
- Ministers don't even try to get to know us before they come in and change everything.
- Ministers say that I have a spiritual problem if I disagree with what's going on in the church.
- Ministers can't be trusted.
- Ministers come to our church so they can climb the ladder to a bigger church.
- Ministers don't love us.
- Ministers manipulate their congregations.

Of course, some of the comments have been biased by frustration, but many of them can be supported with facts. As hard as it is to believe, ministers can get themselves into serious trouble in their churches simply because they don't work on good relational skills.

Chad had been taught well at seminary. He thought he knew all of the ways to grow a healthy church. In his first full-time church, he would put them into practice. And he did, but things didn't go as well as he hoped. In fact, some of the church leaders accused him of not caring for his congregation.

He asked himself how such a charge could be true. He was making what he thought were some good organizational changes. He had calculated the growth potential and set in motion some strategies to meet his growth goals. How could anyone accuse him of not caring?

Then he saw what he was doing. While he was busy with his organizational restructuring, some of his people suffered through their troubles without their minister. While he was preaching his series of sermons that had been designed to accommodate his growth strategy, his people remained spiritually hungry.

They knew what he was talking about, but they didn't know why he was talking about it.

Did Chad make radical changes in his strategy? No, he simply took a little more time with it. And he devoted more of his time to his people. Time took care of the rest of his problem. Once the congregation saw his heart as he cared for them, they trusted him to lead them. And they warmed up to his family too.

The Joy Makers

Working with folks in a congregation can break your heart. Although it's a little painful, talking about the sorrows can help you prepare for them. On the other hand, talking about the things that bring joy to your heart in your relationships with the people in your church can be a lot of fun. We know about them almost instinctively. These gifts from God constantly fuel the fire of our passion for ministry, and they always come wrapped in the package of people.

In the previous section, all of the names of the people involved were changed. The names have also been changed in the stories about Debbie and Susan and the Stevens family that you are about to read. But the names have not been changed in the stories about Dub, Billy and Lucille, Wallace Ann, and Roy. As you will see as you read their stories, changing their names isn't necessary.

Ministers enjoy the thrill of being used by the Lord to make an eternal difference in the lives of people. Today Susan has her head on straight because a minister at a church in her neighborhood happened to be in the office the day she came in desperately searching for help. Debbie, the minister in the office, met her at the door, listened to her, prayed with her, and befriended her. The relationship that began in the church office carried Susan a long way toward wholeness in Christ. She became a Christian, and she learned to walk with Jesus as she raised her two children by herself. When Debbie gets discouraged because of the problems, all she has to do is to reflect on the way the Lord allowed her to make a difference in Susan's life.

Ministers get to know the joy of being loved by people in their congregations. Dub showed his love by making regular trips to a mountain spring just to get water for his pastor. He claimed that it was the best water in the country. His pastor considered each delivery of Dub's special water a gift of love from a quiet Christian man.

Billy and Lucille demonstrated their love for their minister's family one night by driving over to the parsonage in the middle of a hailstorm. They had become worried about their minister's wife, who was alone while her husband was out of town. The hailstorm ruined the windshield of their car, but it didn't matter. As far as Billy and Lucille were concerned, the only thing that mattered was the safety of their minister's family.

Wallace Ann showed her love for her minister's family in ways that constantly surprised everybody in the parsonage. She faithfully wrote thoughtful notes to encourage them, invited them to her house for dinner, and sent them little gifts along the way. And she listened.

Ministers have the joy of involving their families in their work. After Roy died, his son talked about his dad's work as a pastor. Unlike other children who didn't know very much about what their dads did for a living, he got to see his dad minister to people every day. In fact, he said that everybody in their home was involved in some way in his dad's ministry. It was sort of like a family business, only better. They worked hard together, but not to make money. They worked to reach people for Christ. You could say the entire family worked together to lay up heavenly treasure.[1]

Ministers enjoy the privilege of not being strangers in a new community. When the Stevens family moved into their new community to serve a church there, everybody already knew them. Because of their notoriety, they didn't have to face many of the difficulties related to transitioning to a new place. For instance, their children didn't go to school as complete strangers. Many of the teachers and the students knew them and tried hard to help them get settled into their new school. As you can imagine, they came home from school that first day absolutely elated. The people there had treated them like friends who had come home, not strangers who had just moved into the community.

Ministry has its ups and downs, and a minister's family faces the ebbs and flows of congregational life together. The problems that come your way may break your heart. Of course, you have to deal with the problems. At the same time, don't forget to enjoy the people. Over time church buildings will crumble, growth strategies will change, and end-of-the-year statistics will be forgotten. But the relationships that you and your family nurture with your people will last a lifetime. And beyond.

CHAPTER 11

Dining Etiquette

Rhonda H. Kelley

Eating is an important activity of life, not just for survival but for social interaction. While many people enjoy food, Christians love to eat! In fact, fellowship is often defined as food—dinner on the grounds, potluck suppers, ice cream parties, coffee and donuts. Food is a staple of the church. Many churches even call the mid-week meal "Wednesday Night Fellowship." Interaction around the table is healthy and is essential to a happy life. Just as mealtimes are a focal point of family life in the home, fellowship around the table is central to the family of God. Therefore, Christians should learn how to conduct themselves properly when eating.

Many ministers find themselves around the table often. It has been jokingly said that "no preacher ever preaches against gluttony." Most preachers do love to eat—and they like to eat food other than fried chicken. As a guest in another church, the minister often is taken out to eat. As a host, the pastor or staff member may take a visitor to a restaurant or invite him or her to a meal at home. A common practice among churches is an interview around the table. When seeking a new leader, the Pastor Search Committee may take the prospective candidate to dinner. The personnel committee may interview a staff candidate around the table. First impressions while eating are lasting! Since food is so important, ministers should learn how to eat properly. Dining etiquette may actually contribute to the call of a church.

In this article I will review the meaning of etiquette and discuss some dining guidelines before, during, and after the meal. The purpose of this chapter is not to emphasize the unessential or focus too minutely on rules. Instead, the goal is to facilitate an understanding of basic etiquette protocol so that you will feel comfortable in any dining setting. Our conduct at all times is a reflection on the Lord and can bring honor or dishonor to Him. There will be many opportunities for fellowship around the table. As poet laureate Maya Angelou has said, "Life is a glorious banquet, a limitless and delicious buffet." We must dine in comfort and with class so negative attention will not be drawn to us, but positive focus will be directed to Him.

Etiquette

The word *etiquette* actually means "the conduct or procedure required by good breeding or prescribed by authority to be observed in social life."[1] It is a French word from the mid-eighteenth century which implies a set of rules or customs generally accepted in particular cultural groups or social situations.[2] Etiquette is not meant to be legalism or laws, but general guidelines for appropriate behavior. It is simply a special word for getting along with others. We must be careful not to consider *etiquette* just a term that some people think applies only to fancy situations. According to Sue Fox, "Etiquette is often regarded as something you turn on and off for special occasions. But that just isn't so!"[3] While rules of courtesy have changed over time, these gentle guidelines should be learned and followed in our society today.

Christians should look to the Bible for a code of conduct. In the Old Testament, instructions were given for eating. The Book of Leviticus lists unclean and clean foods as well as the feasts of celebration. God gave specific guidelines about what and when and how to eat. Mealtimes were important times for instruction and fellowship. The Virtuous Woman nurtured her family as she provided nutritious meals and sweet fellowship around the table.[4] The New Testament includes stories set in the context of eating meals and gives insights into hospitality.[5] Jesus Himself often visited with people during a meal. He ate in the home of Zacchaeus as well as Mary and Martha of Bethany.[6]

In His ministry, Jesus Christ often ate with His disciples, other followers, and even the unchurched. He hosted a banquet, fed the multitudes, told parables of meals, and gathered at the table for His Last Supper. Certainly He was aware of acceptable behavior, and He desired to be a good example for those around Him. Baptist ministers today will find much of their ministry taking place around the table. Therefore, it is important for them to be familiar with proper dining etiquette so that they will be comfortable in any setting and will present a positive image for themselves, the church, and the Lord.

Before the Meal

As people gather around the table and the meal begins, several important tips should be remembered. These considerations will help everyone feel more comfortable and will make the occasion a pleasant one for all.

If you are the host or hostess, confidently welcome the guests and lead them throughout the meal. The host or hostess should determine the seating arrangement and guide guests to their chairs. Introductions should be made, and a blessing for the food can be spoken aloud.

If you have invited special guests to lunch or dinner, give them the best seats at the table. Let your guests sit facing the crowd of diners. Give them the "banquette" seat against the wall. As host, you may sit next to your guests or opposite them to encourage conversation throughout the meal.

If place cards designate seats at the table, it is extremely impolite to rearrange the seating. A host or hostess has given careful thought to the seating arrangement. Sometimes couples are seated together and other times they are seated separately.

As a guest, always wait for the host or hostess to take his or her seat before you take yours. All signals throughout the event should be from the host or hostess and followed by all guests.

A man should help a woman be seated. Seat the woman sitting to your right. Keep in mind that "the right rules" in our society. Almost all movement and placement are to the right.

Approach the chair from the right, sit to the left. If all people at the table move to the right, confusion and contact are avoided.

Sit one hand span from the table. The space between your body and the table will allow comfortable movement without too much distance for food to travel to your mouth. Sit up straight, with your arms held near your body.

Pick up your napkin after the host or hostess. Place the fold of your napkin to the waist and blot your mouth on the corner of the napkin. Placement of the napkin in your lap actually signals to all guests and to any wait staff that the meal has begun.

These common courtesies will help the meal experience to move smoothly. Awkward moments among guests also will be eliminated.

During the Meal

It is important to remember that a meal is not just for eating; it also is a time for socialization. Try to keep a balance between enjoying your food and enjoying your companions. Keep these pointers in mind during the meal.

Food is served from the left, removed from the right. Be aware of the serving of dishes so you do not accidentally bump the server or spill the food. Movement comes from the left to avoid the right hand, which may be lifting a glass.

Liquids are poured from the right. The server may reach over your right shoulder to pour your beverage. Sometimes the glass is removed so that pouring is handled away from the table. Be aware of the server's position in order to avoid accidents.

The guest of honor is always served first. Ladies should be served before gentlemen, and the host or hostess should be served last.

Wait until the host or hostess begins eating to start your own meal. If the entrée is hot or the dessert is cold, the host or hostess may verbally encourage guests to begin eating. A guest should never begin eating without guidance from the host.

Everyone should be served before anyone starts eating. Each course should be presented to the entire table at once, and plates should not be removed until everyone has completed the course.

When not in use, always keep your napkin in your lap. Put your napkin on your chair if you leave the table, and leave the napkin on the table when the meal is complete. The position of your napkin communicates nonverbally to the server your status during the meal. Do not crumple your napkin when you finish eating.

If you need to leave the table, say softly "Please excuse me." No additional explanation is necessary. Quietly leave the table and return without comment so that conversation is not interrupted.

If you need something on the table, say "Please pass the _____," or *"May I please have the _____ ?"* Do not reach across someone else's place setting. Try to pass all food and condiments before eating begins so there is no disturbance during the meal. The person nearest the item should pass it carefully.

Always pass the condiments (salt, pepper, butter, sugar, etc.) that are in front of you to the right. Pass salt and pepper together, butter and knife together, and so forth. All guests at the table should pass dishes to the right, in the same direction. When you are passing the condiments, do not use them as they are on the way to the person who requested them. Do not season your food before tasting it.

Use your flatware from the outside in. Start with the salad fork or soup spoon which is farthest from the plate and work your way inward, using one utensil for each course.

When eating soup, scoop out, wiping the soup against the rim; then eat. Sip from the side of the spoon for thin soup, or spoon into the mouth for chunky soup. Tip the bowl out when necessary. When eating soup, be careful not to slurp or make any audible sounds. Do not blow on hot soup. Simply allow it to cool to room temperature.

After using a utensil, place it on a plate, not on the table or tablecloth. Be careful not to soil a tablecloth with food on a utensil. The fork or knife can be placed on the plate, and the spoon on the saucer or coaster. The knife's cutting edge should face the diner, and the fork may be placed with the tines up or down.

Hold your utensils like a pencil. Do not grasp them awkwardly or too tightly. Continental- or European-style dining places utensils in opposite hands. When possible, adapt to the cultural setting.

When cutting food, do not saw back and forth. Lift and cut. Cut one bite at a time. The vigorous movement of the knife might shake the table or make a noise on the plate. If only one bite is cut, the remainder of the meat can be shared or taken home.

Break off one bite of bread at a time. Do not butter the entire roll and bite off of it. Butter only the bite-sized piece and put it in your mouth. This keeps your hand and face clean.

When possible, order foods that are easy to eat. Some foods such as french fries, potato chips, or olives can be eaten with the fingers. The "rule of thumb" is neatness.

Do not put your elbows on the table. Leaning on the table is too casual for dining out or with guests. Keep your hands in your lap or on the table when not eating.

Do not blow your nose or cough at the table. Excuse yourself to the bathroom so you do not disturb the guests. Always be considerate of others.

Do not pick your teeth at the table. If something gets stuck in your teeth, excuse yourself and handle it privately.

Table Conversations

The success of a dinner party often will be determined by the enthusiasm of conversation around the table. When people are enjoying themselves, there will be lots of chatter about varied topics. However, keep in mind that table talk should not be loud and boisterous when dining in a restaurant. It is rude to disturb other guests. As a host or hostess, you should try to keep the conversation flowing and to involve every guest in talking. Try not to monopolize the conversation personally. Keep these conversational guidelines in mind as the meal progresses.

Avoid subjects that could ruin one's appetite, offend someone, or depress everyone. Mealtime with guests should include only discussion of pleasant topics—family, travel, and books, for example. Many people believe topics such as politics and religion should be avoided.

Highly personal subjects, your physical ailments, gossip, or topics that are of interest to only a few should also be avoided. The purpose of table talk is to involve all guests. Some conversation will focus on the person seated next to you while other topics will include the entire table. Talk to the person on your right and left and across from you if it is a large party.

Do not talk at length about yourself. The focus of conversation should be others, not yourself. Think about questions that you can ask to draw others into the conversation.

Do not talk "shop" at great lengths to the exclusion of others seated near you. If your meal includes mostly people from the same walk of life, you may discuss business. But try not to devote all the conversation to work. Keep the interests of all guests in mind.

Monitor your participation in the conversation. If you finish eating before others, you have not talked enough. If you have not finished eating, you are talking too much. The goal is for all guests at the table to complete the meal at the same time. A meal in courses should help pace the progress.

Do not talk with food in your mouth. Not only is it unpleasant, but it also rushes the meal. Slow down—chew and swallow first, then talk.

After the Meal

As the meal is finished, the host or hostess will signal time for departure. Final comments can be made as guests exit. Remember these pointers after the meal has been eaten.

It is not proper to push the plate away when you have finished eating. Leave your plate where it is for the server to remove.

All plates should be removed at the same time, when everyone has completed the meal. When eating in a home, feel free to offer to clear the table. However, follow the lead of the host or hostess.

Place your flatware across your plate at the ten-twenty position when you are finished. The used utensils should be placed together diagonally across the plate. This notifies the server that you have completed your meal. Generally speaking, utensils placed in no specific spot means "I'm still eating." Utensils placed to the sides of the plate mean "I want more food." And utensils placed at ten-twenty mean "I'm finished."

Do not stack your dishes when you have finished eating. Leave your dishes in place for the server to remove. Some hostesses prefer not to stack dishes or may have a personal system for clearing the table. Do not be pushy, but be available.

Place your napkin to the left of the plate when the meal has concluded. Not only does this signal completion of the meal, but it keeps the napkin out of the food.

Stand from the table only when the host or hostess stands. This signals the end of the meal and the appropriate time to leave the table.

Be sure to express appreciation for the meal. A verbal and written thank you for a meal is definitely appropriate. You may also want to take a small gift for the host or hostess (flowers, candy, or another token).

Biblical hospitality can be practiced around the table. As a host or hostess, you extend hospitality as you welcome guests and feed them. As an invited guest, your presence and participation uplift and encourage others. The Bible teaches that hospitality is a spiritual gift of ministry to others.[7] It is the unselfish act of sharing what you have and who you are with whomever God sends. It is much more than elegant menus, elaborate table settings, or lavish entertainment. Biblical hospitality is serving others through fellowship. *Koinonia,* the Greek word translated "fellowship," emphasizes building relationships and brings honor to God.

Christian hospitality is not like worldly entertaining. It is not for show or selfish gain. Like hospitality, dining etiquette focuses on others. If you are aware of basic protocol, you will be confident and will help put others at ease. The attention then will be on honored guests, and the glory will be given to the Lord.[8]

Three Commandments of Dining Etiquette

- Always follow the lead of the host or hostess.
- Always use your flatware from the outside in.
- Always be aware of proper etiquette, but adapt to the particular situation.

NOBTS President's Home Table Place Setting

CHAPTER 12

Singleness and Ministry

Jane Bishop

He asked me to marry him. I said yes. It was the way life was expected to be for a young person of the time: grow up, go to college, get married, have children. My wedding had been "planned" since my senior year of high school. Naturally, some of the participants had changed. But now, at the age of twenty-seven, I was going to finalize those wedding plans. This moment was expected to be a highlight of my life.

There was one problem. For several weeks following this proposal of marriage, I was miserable and felt no internal peace. Since life was going exactly as expected, I was caught off balance with these feelings. I would read my Bible and ask God such questions as: "Is he the right one?" "Is there a reason we should not be married?" "Why am I feeling this way?" On some days, a ping-pong match seemed to be taking place in my head.

I knew I loved this man like no other person I had known. I had dated since junior high school and simply thought I had not discovered the "right one" for me until now. I had never even considered not getting married someday. I did not know I could consider it as an option. I had not been in any environment that discussed singleness as a possibility for one's life. So it was not on my list of questions to discuss with God initially.

Weeks passed with no answer. I finally asked God if marriage was what He wanted for my life. It was then He answered. It wasn't a question of whether this was the right man for me. It was a question of what God wanted for my life versus what was assumed would be my life.

As I realized God's plan for me was not marriage, I had a decision to make. I could commit to God's plan and remain single, or I could follow what culture assumed was the plan: grow up, go to college, get married, and have children. When I chose to commit to God's plan on a day in 1983, I felt an immediate sense of peace. I had been approaching God trying to analyze why I was feeling miserable and restless. It was only when I was willing to ask what He intended for me that the answer became clear: I was to be single.

Choosing singleness or marriage is a decision Christians must make in concert with God. However, singleness is rarely discussed as an option. It is not taught. It is rarely modeled. Introducing singleness as an option for one's life does not imply that marriage is bad. It simply recognizes that God may be calling some to be single, and those He is calling need an environment that gives "permission" to explore this option with God. Singleness may be for a season in life or for a lifetime. That is between God and the individual.

Singleness can be challenging, but then being married can be challenging. Each simply has a different set of challenges. One of the challenges of singleness is often being misunderstood. Since the expectation of culture, both secular and church, is that individuals will marry, it is often assumed that if a person remains single or becomes single, there is a problem. They certainly must be gay or emotionally disturbed or just too particular in finding a mate. And if their spouse has died, why haven't they remarried? After all, God created Adam and saw that it was not good for him to be alone.[1] So how could singleness be good?

Although these verses in Genesis have been used appropriately to refer to marriage, there could be broader implications, according to J. Clark Hensley in *Good News for Today's Singles*. Hensley notes that God "created each of us for loving relationships whether or not we ever marry. God created us for relationship and not aloneness."[2] It is aloneness that is not good. And that can be experienced even in marriage relationships.

In his book *Singling, A New Way to Live the Single Life,* John R. Landgraf defines singlehood as "a condition of encouraging, affirming, and maintaining one's integrity as a self."[3] He also notes that healthy, whole singlehood still involves relationships, "otherwise its value would be meaningless."[4] God created humans as relational beings, and being single does not reduce the need for a relational lifestyle. When God called me to be single, He did not ask me to remove myself from people and relationships. He asked me to relate out of the context of singleness.

Another challenge unique to being single is navigating in a "couples world." This expectation begins being reinforced as a child when comments such as "when you grow up and get married" and "when you get married and have children" are usually a consistent part of a person's life. Church culture continually perpetuates this challenge too. The emphasis is consistently on the "traditional family": husband, wife, and children. This implies that people who have a status other than "traditional family" are not important. I have often observed the following behavior. When people enter a church environment (worship, Bible study, etc.) for the first time and are with someone, they are approached and welcomed. Those who enter the same environment alone often are not approached or welcomed for some time, if ever. When a person is not paired with someone (spouse, parent, friend, etc.), it is as if he or she is invisible.

Phrases used for conversation starters also perpetuate the challenge of navigating in a "couples world": "What does your husband/wife do?" "How many children do you have?" When someone is dating, the typical question is usually "When is the marriage date?" After the marriage, "When are you going to have children?" People often assume I am married. One of the first questions I usually am asked is "How many children do you have?" When my reply was "None because I am not married," the conversation often stalled. I have learned to use a different response that usually disarms any awkwardness the other person may be feeling. My reply now is "I have none because I choose not to have children without a husband." That usually gets a chuckle and helps put the other person more at ease. Most of the time, the conversation continues by finding other "starters."

As I have observed people in different settings, I have learned that many married couples are simply not comfortable in relating to singles. They may be intimidated by a single of any definition (never married, single again, etc.). Married people often think they have nothing in common with singles. Or they think if their marriage is intact, it will remind a single parent of a failed marriage. People who are married may feel threatened by singles. Singles can also contribute to this awkwardness. When an individual is not comfortable with being single (either for a season or for a lifetime), relationships can be affected.

Churches must confront the fact that "traditional family" is no longer the norm of today's culture. How many singles of any definition are unreached because they don't have the "traditional credentials"? Statistics show that singleness is more a lifestyle than ever before. Divorce rates for first marriages doubled to 43 percent between 1960 and 1980. Now the divorce rate is approximately 50 percent for first marriages and 60 percent for second marriages. "But in 'Bible-Belt' states where the church has a tradition of powerful influence, the divorce rate is more than 50% above the national norm. . . ."[5] If a unique challenge for singles is navigating in a "couples world," what are churches doing to provide guidance and navigation tools?

Certainly not all are single by God's plan. But God created everyone. The psalmist said of God, "I will praise thee; for I am fearfully and wonderfully made; marvellous are thy works" (Ps. 139:14). Another common observation is that "God doesn't make any junk." What will it take for Christians to reach out to people because they are God's creation, not because of their marital status? When Jesus commands us to love one another as He loved us,[6] there is no status attached—only a statement with a period.

A third challenge to singleness is dealing with myths. I have observed and experienced three that seem to occur consistently: a person who is single is incomplete, a person who is single has more time than married couples, and a person who is single has no life. When churches fall into the trap of these and other myths, ministry with singles is greatly affected. I will comment on these three in an attempt to shatter these myths.

MYTH: A person who is single is incomplete.

FACT: Marriage does not guarantee completeness or wholeness. Neither does singleness. Completeness comes out of a relationship with Jesus Christ. Salvation has to do with wholeness. When we think of salvation only in terms of spiritual deliverance, the purpose of wholeness can be overlooked. When God saved us, He called us to wholeness. "Wholeness means to allow the true self within each person to emerge, to be known, to have its own existence in Christ affirmed."[7]

I have been blessed with parents who have always encouraged me to be the person Christ wants me to be. My parents have never placed any pressure on me to marry. Their training and support have always focused on discovering what God wants for my life and following Him. As I have talked with many singles through the years, I have discovered such encouragement by parents is rare. There is usually much pressure, direct and indirect, to marry.

MYTH: A person who is single has more time than married couples.

FACT: When God created day and night,[8] He didn't stipulate that days would be longer for someone who is single. There are twenty-four hours in a day. A person's marital status does not add or subtract hours. What singles may experience is more flexible discretionary time. If there is not a spouse or children to care for, singles may choose to commit their time differently than someone who has a spouse and children. More discretionary time may not be available for single parents. However, the fact still remains there are twenty-four hours in a day—no more, no less.

MYTH: A person who is single has "no life."

FACT: Jesus came that "they might have life, and that they might have it more abundantly."[9] A person's marital status may dictate what elements are in his or her life. But a life is made full through Jesus Christ, not marital status. Singles may choose to withdraw from people and relationships. However, this is usually more an issue of how they are dealing with themselves. Many singles have not developed tools to navigate in a "couples world." The easy way of dealing with this paired environment is to give an appearance of "no life." Where is the forum for singles to express their needs and receive the "tools" to deal with those needs? Where is the forum for them to learn about abundant living?

My journey as a single has been and continues to be fulfilling. My value as a person and my contentment with life are grounded in my relationship with Jesus Christ. I am complete and whole through Him. I don't wake up each morning and immediately think of being single. In fact, the way I view my marital status is similar to the way I view my age. I don't think about it until someone asks. God has gifted me to be single, so it is not an issue. I can relate to people out of my relationship with Jesus Christ, not out of my marital status. I firmly believe God created me in His image.[10] And if it is good, who am I to question God about it?

When I invited Jesus to become a part of my life at age eight, I had no idea what that decision would mean as I grew older. I knew only as much as an eight-year-old child could comprehend. Likewise, when I chose to follow God's plan for my life of being single, I had no idea what that decision would mean. As I look back at the journey with Him to this point in my life, I see that He has led me along pathways that required a single person. This affirms my calling to singleness.

I have never looked back on the decision to answer God's call on my life to be single and asked God "Why me?" It is one of those life decisions that I willingly made. God has blessed me with His complete assurance that being single is His plan for me. I am single by choice, not by default!

I know now that answering God's call to singleness requires a willingness to risk being different from what culture expects. It requires acting on a strong faith in Jesus Christ. It requires the willingness to live in a "couples world" without apologizing for one's calling. I also know that God's call is individual. What

He has called and gifted me for in life is His plan for me. Each Christian must take responsibility for seeking God's call and direction for his or her life. Although God seems to call most people into a marriage relationship, how many people marry because of what is expected by culture rather than what God has planned for their life? Church leaders must be willing to recognize and accept that God calls individuals as He chooses. And when God's calling goes against human expectations, it must not be deemed insignificant. Leaders enter dangerous waters when they try to assume the role of God.

My experiences as a single in ministry have been positive. That does not mean there have not been challenges, disappointments, and heartaches; life experiences happen regardless of marital status. But it does mean that I don't feel the need to comment constantly on my singleness. I am a Christian who happens to be called to be single.

There is a television commercial that shows a man going through the day telling everyone he meets that he has lowered his cholesterol. He seems to feel the need to give that information even on an elevator! I don't feel the need to go around constantly commenting on my calling as a single. However, when God prompts, I will speak clearly. I recall the first time He "prompted" me to verbalize my call to singleness. I was part of a singles panel in one of my seminary classes. The purpose of the panel was to discuss unique stressors for singles. One student finally asked if any of us had been called to be single. When I raised my hand, the class went into freeze-frame! My response was so foreign they didn't know how to respond. It was another reminder that singleness is not often discussed and certainly is not taught as a viable option for one's life.

When God called me into the ministry in February 1986, I never questioned whether He could use me as a single. I simply heard His calling and chose to respond. Responding to God's call is the easy part. Living it out is the challenge. But as long as I keep my eyes on Jesus, I can run "the race that is set before [me]."[11] A friend shared Zephaniah 3:17 with me recently as an encouragement. What my friend did not know was that verse has been one of my life Scriptures since September 2, 1982. I have it dated in my Bible and remember clearly the day and the circumstances in which God first used it in my life. I was extremely frustrated with my career then (coaching/teaching) and feeling very discouraged and alone. As I was sitting in my office looking for some direction from God, He gave me Zephaniah 3:17: "The LORD thy God in the midst of thee is mighty; he will save, he will rejoice over thee with joy; he will rest in his love, he will joy over thee with singing." Since that day almost twenty years ago, He has used that verse many times to encourage me, to quiet my soul, and to remind me that He rejoices over my life.

Singleness and ministry is an option. It is a calling by God. Consider the following for further discussion.

- How can strong Christian singles be used in leadership roles?
- How can church leaders help create a forum for individuals to explore God's call on their life?
- Use non-traditional conversation starters. Ask different individuals for examples.
- Relate to people as individuals first. Discover who they are, what their interests are, and what God is doing in their life. Allow their marital status to be secondary.
- Who are the singles in your church, and how is God using them?
- Brainstorm with a group of singles about ways to break the myths of singleness.
- Provide an environment that allows singles to express and deal with their unique needs.
- Help singles develop the "tools" they need to navigate in a "couples world."
- Recognize that singleness is a gift, whether for a season or for a lifetime. Affirm those who believe God is calling them into singleness.
- Recognize that singles are individuals who deal with different life issues (i.e., never married, single again without children, single again with children, senior adult single again, etc.).

CHAPTER 13

Being a Minister's Wife: A Testimony

Carol Lemke

I would like to share with you my Christian pilgrimage from the perspective of a minister's wife. I will not be able to give you solutions for all the unique challenges of a minister's family life, but I hope you will benefit from some of the lessons I have learned in my experience.

I grew up in a Christian home in a Bible-Belt town and was involved in the activities of a Southern Baptist church every time the doors were open. I graduated from a Baptist college with a music degree and have tried to stay in the center of God's will for my life as long as I can remember.

I met my husband, Steve, when he came to serve for the summer in my home church, and God revealed to us in just a few short weeks that we were to be life partners. We married a year later, and I began my journey as a partner in the ministry that God had planned for us.

During this journey God has given me the opportunity of serving in several different roles—as a seminary student's wife, a pastor's wife, a college and seminary faculty member's wife, and now as a seminary administrator's wife. Each time I have put on a new and different hat, I have asked God why He has chosen this role for me; and each time He has revealed to me why He wanted me to be where He has put me. Sometimes it has taken me a while to understand and accept these changing roles, but as He has led me through each of these times, I have learned more and more about faith and have been reminded that God always wants the very best for me.

When Steve and I married, he was beginning the Ph.D. program at Southwestern Baptist Theological Seminary, and I had my first *major* move—from North Carolina, the land of my birth and where all my family lived, to some strange land called Texas. Our first home was in a "furnished" (and I use that word loosely) seminary apartment in a not-so-wonderful neighborhood. We were financially challenged and ate a lot of beans and rice before we knew that was a good thing. But we were surrounded by other seminary student couples and developed some lifelong friendships as we shared student life together.

In retrospect I will tell you that this was probably one of the easiest campsites in my journey. I don't suppose it really seemed easy when I was in the middle of it, but I was young and very much in love with an incredible young man who had committed himself to God for full-time ministry. What a thought! Steve was a full-time student, and I was a full-time supporter of his task. I supported him by working full time so he could concentrate on accomplishing his goal. However, his goal had now become *our* goal, so I prayed that God would use me to allow Steve's attention to be focused on his studies.

During this time we sought God's will for His timetable about starting a family. Our friends who had children during their time at seminary expressed to us their frustrations and struggles because they did not have the time or financial resources that they would have liked to provide for their family. We believed that we should wait until Steve finished seminary before we had children. God gave us a little more than a year while immersed in the doctoral program to live in a seminary apartment, be newlyweds, and grow together in all areas of our lives as a married couple.

Through this year of seeking God's will for our lives, we began the process—for the first time, but definitely not the last—of looking for a church for my husband to pastor. This was a major learning experience for me; I had *never* done anything like this before. To be evaluated by a group of people who spent a few short hours getting to know us, for Steve to be evaluated by preaching one sermon . . . well, that didn't seem to be quite fair. On the other hand, Steve and I had to do some evaluating ourselves. After being involved in a large church in my hometown in North Carolina, I had adjusted pretty well to being a member of a large church in Texas, but I had never seen anything like some of the little Texas churches in little Texas towns. God walked us through this experience—being "rejected" by a church, knowing this was not a personal rejection but rather not the place where God wanted us to serve, and also gracefully declining to serve in a place *we* believed was not where God wanted us to serve.

One of the interesting experiences I had during this process was noting a particular look in the eyes of members of a search committee when they learned this potential pastor had a wife who could play the piano. *Every* time we talked with a committee, Steve explained very tactfully that this was not a "buy one, get one free" situation. With every search committee we always discussed *their* expectations of the role of the pastor's wife. This allowed me to assume church responsibilities in light of God's leadership—and not the pressure of church members—to use the gifts God has given me in the appropriate way and at the appropriate time. I know you will want to protect your family from being forced into the role expectations of others as you seek God's leadership in ministry positions.

After several months of some tears and some laughter, Steve accepted the position of pastor at a church in west Texas where about seventy-five ranchers, farmers, and a few local businessmen along with their families gathered for worship on Sunday. We invested our lives in that church and its people, and we still have relationships with many of them twenty years later.

During the five years of serving this congregation of God's people and three years of serving another Texas congregation, I learned a lot about being a pastor's wife.

- I learned that playing the piano in a small church in a small town in west Texas was different from accompanying the youth choir in my home church. (Yes, I eventually *volunteered* to be the church pianist and enjoyed every minute of it!) This was all about adapting to a different worship style and being out of my comfort zone. However, I learned not only to appreciate how these people worshiped but also that I could worship with them.

- I encountered church business meetings that were like no other church business meetings I had ever known. Out of this experience I came to understand that not everybody is happy all the time, and that sometimes some church members did not agree with their pastor, my husband. I learned not to take it personally; these folks were still my Christian brothers and sisters.

- I discovered that hospitality was not only about being a hostess but also graciously receiving hospitality in homes that were different from my own.

- While I felt the need to develop some close friendships and confidants, I realized the importance of establishing relationships with as many individuals as possible—the lovely and the unlovely. I found that sometimes I needed to take the initiative to get to know people who had not necessarily made the effort themselves to get to know me. God did give us some special relationships within that congregation.

- We both realized the importance of having relationships outside of the church congregation and outside of that small town. Of course you cannot discuss one church member with another; they probably are related to each other, either by blood or by marriage. We learned the importance of being involved with the other ministers in the local Baptist association. We, as ministers and wives serving God in the same geographical area, served as a very important support group for one another.

Being a minister's wife is a very demanding role. Please remember to be supportive of your spouse in his or her "unpaid" position. Steve has always given me that support and has always been very affirming of me—in public and, most important, in our home.

Our next ministry position presented both of us with a number of role changes and cultural adjustments. God led us to a small Baptist college in rural northeast Arkansas where Steve served as a faculty member. The more relaxed role expectations of a faculty member's wife allowed me the opportunity to develop as an individual outside of my role as Steve's wife. I had opportunity to use my musical gifts both inside and outside the church. I became involved in several community activities, and I learned the value of civic involvement as a Christian. We became involved in the lives of people whose backgrounds and values were often very different from ours. I gained self-confidence during this time, and God used this ministry as a building block to prepare me for future roles in other places.

It was during this period in our lives that we (notice the word *we*) decided it was time to start our family so we could have two children while we were still reasonably young. We had been married for seven years, Steve had finally completed his doctoral studies and had a full-time position, and we had bought a home. The timing seemed perfect. This was the beginning of a journey of learning patience, faith, and God's timing. This walk lasted for seven years while we sought out the assistance of fertility specialists and cried out to God at the injustice of it all. We would be great parents—didn't God realize that?

By the way, it is difficult to understand totally the heartbreak of infertility if you have not experienced it yourself. As you minister to couples who are dealing with this problem, give them all the compassion you can; but it is important to encourage them to become a part of a support group, either organized or informal.

We learned to pray for God's timing and for His will concerning our family. I can't say that now, being on the other side of this experience, I understand fully why God chose this path for us; but I do know that through this experience I have had unique opportunities to share God's love. I *know* that God has planned the very best for us. God led us to good doctors, and after fourteen years of marriage I became pregnant with our child. Austin was born in August 1992.

Steve was a faculty member at Southwestern Seminary when

Austin was born. He was following God's leadership to make a difference in people's lives through seminary education and was doing so at the institution where he had been taught and mentored. Physically and emotionally we settled into our suburban Fort Worth home and began planning Austin's life—choosing preschools and other educational opportunities for our "exceedingly bright" son—while nurturing friendships and relationships in the seminary community, our church community, and our neighborhood. All was well.

Then one day Steve came home and told me that the president of New Orleans Baptist Seminary had called him and asked him if we would pray about becoming provost at that institution. After asking Steve to explain what a provost does, I felt assured that God did not want us to leave our comfortable life in Texas and raise our son in New Orleans! (We didn't know anyone who lived there.) After extensive interviews and a visit to the campus, Steve felt God was giving him an opportunity to affect His Kingdom in an even greater way through helping to shape the academic programs of a Southern Baptist institution. However, he would not accept the position until I consented to make the move.

I prayed and cried and prayed some more, but I could not understand why God was doing this to us. I was concerned about Steve's being in an administrative position when he was such an excellent teacher. I was concerned about living and raising a child in New Orleans. I prayed that God would give me the clear direction and the peace that Steve had, but it did not come. Steve was being very patient with me, but there came a time when a decision had to be made; and, for the first time in our marriage, I had to agree to start a new ministry based on God's leadership in Steve's life without feeling the same call. I am afraid that my own stubborn will was getting in the way of God's will for my life, but I am thankful for His blessings in spite of my stubbornness. Within the first year I knew we were serving Him where He wanted us to be.

As we considered this life-changing move, our almost-five-year-old Austin significantly affected my attitude. I had to choose to present a positive picture to a child who had known no other home and was very much endeared to all the people, places, and things (including Tex-Mex food and the Dallas Cowboys) of his native Texas town. We sought out all the wonderful people, places, and things (maybe not the New Orleans Saints) in our new hometown. And we talked about knowing that God wants the very best for us and about the importance of following His plan for our lives.

We wanted Austin to be a part of this decision. He initially told us that God had told him that we should stay in Fort Worth! Before we made the decision to move, we took him to New Orleans to see the house, neighborhood, and city in which he would live. Austin not only came to accept the decision to move, but he made the transition to life in New Orleans more easily than we did.

Actually, God has used Austin in many ways to help me adjust to our new ministry in New Orleans. Looking at the world, and New Orleans, through a child's eyes brings a fresh perspective of God's love as He inspires me every day to be more bold in my Christian walk. In my search for acceptance as the provost's wife, not wanting to be perceived differently from the faculty wives, I have become known more often as Austin's mother than the provost's wife. I am once again learning to establish my priorities, balancing the ministry to which I feel called as the provost's wife with the importance of putting the needs of my family first. I continue to learn to seek God's leadership in accepting responsibilities; no matter how great the need is, I must determine God's will for my life and for my family's life and not succumb to pressure from outside *nor* the pressure I put on myself to be all things to all people. God entrusted to us the life of a child, and right now he loves his mother and wants me to be involved in his life. And Steve needs me to take care of all the little details in our lives to allow him to spend his free time with his son.

I am often introduced as the provost's wife. (Steve affectionately calls me the "provostess.") But who I truly am is Steve's wife, Austin's mother, and, most important, God's child. And

He is still in the process of shaping and molding me into what He wants me to be.

I realize that I have many new challenges to face in the not-so-distant future. But I know that God will continue to walk with me and will not allow me to face any challenge that He will not equip me to handle. For I know God has a plan for my life that is more blessed than I can possibly imagine.

As the apostle Paul wrote in his prayer for the Ephesian Christians:

> For this cause I bow my knees unto the Father of our Lord Jesus Christ, of whom the whole family in heaven and earth is named, that he would grant you, according to the riches of his glory, to be strengthened with might by his Spirit in the inner man; that Christ may dwell in your hearts by faith; that ye, being rooted and grounded in love, may be able to comprehend with all saints what is the breadth, and length, and depth, and height; and to know the love of Christ, which passeth knowledge, that ye might be filled with all the fulness of God. (Eph. 3:14-19)

PART IV

Your Relationships in Your Church

CHAPTER 14

Emotional Intelligence and Spiritual Maturity
Steve Echols

People Skills Are Critically Important

We have all heard it, or perhaps we have even said it ourselves: "He (or she) is book smart but not people smart." Such a comment is often more than just a cutting remark. Being able to develop and maintain good relationships is essential in any field, but especially in the church. In recent years, research by LifeWay has confirmed that the lack of interpersonal and leadership skills is the major factor in forced termination. No amount of other ministerial talents can adequately compensate for not being able to get along with church members. We all know of individuals who graduated from seminary with a Ph.D. or had exceptional talent but never were successful for this very reason.

Defining "People Skills"

Among the churches, the term people skills often has been used to describe the minister's ability to work effectively with parishioners. This term has been used to describe a plethora of traits. Sometimes this description has brought more confusion than clarity. Does having people skills mean that a person must be highly extroverted, effervescent, charismatic, or just plain have "the gift for gab"?

In recent years some new terms are helping us to understand what we mean when we talk about people skills. In the field of psychology and social behavior one such term is "emotional intelligence" as coined by John Mayer of the University of New Hampshire and Peter Salovey of Yale in 1990.[1] More recently, this designation has been popularized in the writings of Daniel Goleman. He strongly connected emotional intelligence with interpersonal skills. He noted that many people "with IQs of 160 work for people with IQs of 100" because the latter have a higher interpersonal intelligence than the former. Goleman wrote, "In the day-to-day world no intelligence is more important than the interpersonal."[2] Translated into the local church setting, this means that no matter how well ministers preach, teach, organize, give pastoral care, or even how much passion and commitment they have, if they lack emotional or interpersonal intelligence they are not likely to be successful.

Goleman presented a complex case that emotional intelligence is part of the very essence of what it means to be human. He explored the area of the brain called the amygdala, which studies have determined to be the center of emotions. He rejected as utter nonsense that a really intelligent person moves beyond emotion. Instead, emotional intelligence is a vital part of the total picture of human intelligence. A Christian might interpret this data as meaning that God has "hardwired" emotions into the human brain.

Goleman identified five specific areas of emotional intelligence: (1) knowing one's emotions, (2) managing one's emotions, (3) motivating oneself, (4) recognizing emotions in others, and (5) handling relationships.[3] Some connections of these traits to the successful practice of ministry are quite obvious.

The Connection between Emotional Intelligence and Ministry Effectiveness

First, if a minister does not accurately perceive his or her emotional state, the consequences can be serious. The ministry is a profession that evokes a wide variety of emotions. The celebration of a new birth, the preaching of a funeral, and the conducting of a wedding ceremony can all happen in a single day. Moving from situation to situation, ministers may not be readily aware of the emotional residue they are carrying. To be able to understand the state of one's anger, exuberance, or even depression is critically important. Discerning the cycle of emotions can be extremely valuable in preventing the wrong action at the wrong time.

Second, managing emotions is essential. In some cases even a single display of anger has been known to result in termination. One of the most talented staff members I have ever known could not control his anger. Today he is out of the ministry. Likewise, other emotions in addition to anger must be controlled. Every minister who truly cares often feels great sadness and even despair at the depth of human suffering. Yet, ministers cannot let their feelings of melancholy hinder their work. For instance, when ministers are with those who are grieving, they can allow their emotions to help them to connect with the family. Yet, somehow they must maintain control in order to be a source of strength for the family. This is not an easy task, but it is part of emotional intelligence.

Third, motivating oneself is critical in a profession where one must be a self-starter. Where does the minister find the emotional energy for the vast tasks of leading and caring for a church? Burnout is a frequent problem. Recently, a prominent pastor in a very large church resigned. He confided in me about the reason. He felt physically, mentally, and emotionally drained. At mid-career, this pastor is out of local church ministry. This dilemma is not uncommon. After a few years, ministers sometimes discover that they can no longer find the motivation even to attempt the many tasks they face. They feel depleted. Though they are not immune to fatigue, the emotionally intelligent find a way to marshal emotions to provide the energy for the tasks at hand.

Fourth, a minister must recognize emotions in others. Some communication specialists have stated that nonverbal and paralanguage convey as much as 60 to 65 percent of the meaning of a conversation.[4] One of my friends in local church ministry was extremely skillful in many ways. However, he had difficulty picking up on the nonverbal and paralanguage emotional cues. In some instances, he took the words of a person to mean that he or she was supportive of a certain action, when all the nonverbal and paralanguage were giving the opposite message. This contradiction caused him major problems. The minister must recognize that the choice of words may be mere politeness, but the paralanguage and nonverbal language can reveal true feelings.

Finally, in regard to the fifth aspect of emotional intelligence, handling relationships is the bottom line. Without healthy relationships with family members, the congregation, and other constituents, it is nearly impossible to have an effective ministry.

The Relationship between Emotional Intelligence and Spiritual Maturity

Is there any relationship between what Goleman and others call emotional intelligence and what Christians call spiritual maturity? The answer is most emphatically *yes*! How does having spiritual maturity make one emotionally intelligent? Consider the following parallels. First, Goleman maintained that knowing one's emotions or self-awareness is "the keystone of emotional intelligence."[5] The reason is simple. One cannot modify what one does not recognize. One frequent area of denial for ministers is anger.

Many circumstances in ministry can produce anger. Ministers may become frustrated over impossible demands made by unreasonable parishioners. Yet, the resource that the Christian has that the world can never know is the Holy Spirit speaking through prayer, meditation, and the Word of God. The Holy Spirit is said to be the one who brings conviction of sin and who is a guide into all truth.[6] In regard to the efficacy of the Word, the writer of the Book of Hebrews declared, "For the word of God is quick, and powerful, and sharper than any two-edged sword, piercing even to the dividing asunder of soul and spirit, and of the joints and marrow, and is a discerner of the thoughts and intents of the heart."[7] When the Holy Spirit convicts us about our anger, as well as other negative interpersonal conduct and emotional states, we then have the possibility of seeing a positive change.

Other Scriptures are easily applicable to these concepts. According to Goleman, the second aspect of emotional intelligence, managing emotions, "is an ability built on self-awareness."[8] From the Christian viewpoint, the same Holy Spirit who enables us to discern our emotions also enables us to be healthy and whole in our emotions. Perhaps this is what Paul referred to when he stated, "Be ye angry, and sin not."[9] The third aspect, motivating oneself, has much to do with perspective. Goleman observed the connection between motivation and the qualities of hope and optimism.[10] The minister can find motivation by the belief that his labor is making a difference. Paul expressed this thought when he declared, "And let us not be weary in well doing: for in due season we shall reap, if we faint not."[11] From Goleman's viewpoint, the fourth issue of emotional intelligence, recognizing emotions in others, is the quality of empathy. Paul emphasized the quality of empathy when he exhorted Christians to "rejoice with them that do rejoice, and weep with them that weep."[12]

The last aspect of emotional intelligence mentioned by Goleman, handling relationships, has the most obvious connection to spiritual maturity. The heart of Christianity is about relationships. Jesus emphasized this truth when He declared that the foremost commandment is, "Thou shalt love the Lord thy God with all thy heart, and with all thy soul, and with all thy mind."[13] "*Heart, soul,* and *mind*" mean the totality of everything that we have been created to be, including our emotions. Further, Jesus stated that the second commandment "is like unto it, Thou shalt love thy neighbour as thyself."[14] This is, of course, an emphasis on the interpersonal, which is expressed as emotional intelligence.

Unfortunately, ministers sometimes do not recognize the obvious. They do not fully understand the implications of what Jesus said. In one sense, the field of emotional intelligence has made a connection that ministers need to make. Being human is far more than cognitive functions. It always has been and always will be about relationships. First, it has to do with our relationship with God and, from that, our relationship with people. The Christian insight into emotional intelligence is that in loving God and others we are transformed as well as our relationships. Love is emotional intelligence carried to the ultimate level. Yet, it is easy to say that we should all love God and others, but what does it mean specifically? The character Lucy in the Peanuts cartoon once declared, "I love the whole world; it's just people that I can't stand."

Some Neglected Areas That Can Make a Difference

In ministry, I have noticed four key areas that are sometimes overlooked as ways in which church members sense that the minister really loves them. Sometimes it may be the seemingly small things that speak the loudest. Furthermore, they can make the difference between success and failure in the practice of ministry.

First is the area of communication. Real communication is not easy. Ministers often make a mistake in thinking that communication is automatic. Communication studies have revealed that much of the intended message is never received. Due to things like leveling (details are lost), condensing (message is shortened and simplified), sharpening (details are highlighted), assimilation (message is interpreted according to desires and expectations), and embellishing (details are added), communication is never 100 percent.[15] Unfortunately, the tendency is to assume that people deliberately fail to understand us or do not communicate honestly with us. While this failure does occur sometimes, often it is just a matter of human limitations. To communicate requires great effort. James encouraged Christians to be "swift to hear, slow to speak, slow to wrath."[16] Communicating also requires great skill. The writer of Proverbs declared, "Counsel in the heart of man is like deep water; but a man of understanding will draw it out."[17]

In ministry there is always the press for time. However, merely announcing something does not necessarily mean the matter has been communicated. The emotionally intelligent and spiritually mature response is to do whatever it takes to communicate. We can become impatient. If we grow weary of all the trouble it takes to communicate with people, we would do well to remember that God went to a lot of trouble to communicate with us by sending His Son into the world.

Second is the similar issue of availability. The minister's schedule is often made hectic by constant interruptions. It is a difficult challenge to be efficient but also accessible. However, emotional intelligence research reminds us that task accomplishment is important, but relationships with people are even more important. Jesus had the perfect balance. He never strayed from His purpose but always had time for people.

In the practical everyday world of church life, one significant issue is the returning of phone calls and e-mails. I have known a number of ministers in churches of various sizes who have lost credibility with their congregations because they do not return contacts. Ministers should set up a specific time each day to check and make sure they have followed up on messages they have received.

Ministers may think that casual conversation is a waste of time, but often it is an opportunity for ministry. Eugene Peterson emphasized what he called the ministry of small talk. He explained that most people do not go from one crisis to another. Rather, they take part in everyday tasks in which "small talk is the natural language." He added, "If pastors belittle it, we belittle what most people are doing most of the time, and the gospel is misrepresented."[18]

One of the most talented and committed educational ministers I have ever known is no longer in vocational Christian ministry. The reason was not for lack of performance. He was outstanding. If he said he would do something, you could take it to the bank that it would be done with excellence. He had a pleasant personality. He was kind and gracious to people who came to see him. What was the problem? Whenever he walked down the halls of the church, he never looked up. He was shy by nature and very task orientated. Church members did not understand. They took the fact that he did not take time to speak as a neglect of common courtesy. This problem was pointed out to him, but old habits are hard to break. The opposition to his ministry among church members grew, and the ultimate outcome was his resignation. Availability, even in the ministry of small talk, is more important than often imagined.

Third, there is the opportunity for encouragement. On the surface, looking out at the Sunday morning crowd, all appears well. Yet, the minister knows that beneath the surface many of those present are living lives of "quiet desperation." In preaching and teaching opportunities, the therapeutic side of God's Word must never be neglected. The ability to empathize is a sign not only of emotional intelligence but also of spiritual maturity. One of the ways to display empathy is to make people always feel special. A minister would be hard pressed to find a compliment greater than the one spoken by a parishioner: "You know what I like about your ministry? You make everyone feel like they are somebody." In my classes, I always tell students that they should greet and treat each person they meet as though that individual is the King or Queen of England. Such action cannot be effectively faked, but it must come from a genuine attitude from within. It is a concrete way to love people, remembering that they are made in the image of God.[19] True unconditional love is given to each person, no matter how he or she acts.

Finally, another neglected area is acceptance. Emotional intelligence recognizes that people operate from different paradigms. Spiritually speaking this is known as the diversity of gifts.[20] Many different matrixes are used to express categories of diversity. I found that one of the most helpful ways to build a team is for everyone to take a diagnostic test like the *DISC Personal Profile System*.[21] Though tests like these are never 100 percent accurate, they do show how people can genuinely differ in personality and gifts. Many times we assume people are trying to be difficult when in reality they are just expressing the way in which they are different. One of the lessons that I had to learn early in my ministry was that a stronger team could be built if I allowed for diversity. The minister with emotional intelligence and spiritual maturity recognizes the strength of a cross-functional team.

The Good News: We Can Change for the Better

If trying to practice emotional intelligence through spiritual maturity seems overwhelming, there is good news. Quantitative research has shown that people can change the level of their emotional intelligence. Hendrie Weisinger agreed and asserted, "You increase your emotional intelligence by learning and practicing skills and capabilities that make up emotional intelligence."[22] If a secular viewpoint can advocate a position that people can change, then Christians should be ashamed of thinking that believers cannot change. Earlier I gave the example of the minister who could not recognize the nonverbal clues people were giving him. The encouraging part of the story is that when he became aware of this deficiency, he was able to improve greatly in this area.

Christianity is about more than changing the way we act; it is about becoming a new person.[23] There is a supernatural power available to the believer to bring about spiritual maturity. The fruit of the Spirit in the life of the minister can more than fulfill the need for "people skills" or "emotional intelligence."[24] We do not have to feel trapped by past hang-ups and shortcomings in personality and social skills. God's plan is not complex, but instead it is simple. As Paul declared, "Therefore if any man be in Christ, he is a new creature: old things are passed away; behold, all things are become new" (2 Cor. 5:17).

CHAPTER 15

Learning to Relate to Difficult People

Jeanine Cannon Bozeman

Relating to difficult people, all kinds of people, is very important in ministry. Ministers often are dismissed from their churches because they have difficulty relating to people. We can learn to relate to persons if we choose, and improvement in the area of relationships is not only desirable, but necessary.

Learning to relate to difficult people can be a particularly painful task. Most of us know at least one person we would classify as "hard to get along with." That person may be a relative, church member, friend, or acquaintance. In addition, we must acknowledge that all of us tend to be difficult to some people at some time.

Difficult people behave in the way they do because their behavior gets them what they want. The behavior works for them, and they will continue the difficult behavior as long as it does so. Difficult behavior is learned. We cannot change others, but we can learn to be assertive and confront their behavior in order to survive. In other words, we can change our behavior toward difficult people.

When I think of persons considered to be difficult, I am not thinking of persons who are occasionally difficult, but of persons who are habitually and continually difficult. Their behavior is consistently difficult and obnoxious, and they continue such behavior in order to gain or maintain a power position.

Nearly everyone is a problem to somebody, sometime, somewhere. My mother used to say that she could be nice for two

hours, but that was her limit. I often think my duration of nice-
ness is much shorter. I invite you to consider several types of
difficult behavior and how you can deal with them effectively.
Learning to cope with each behavior will not change the person, but it will enable you not to become totally frustrated and
overwhelmed. Consider the following patterns of behavior that
may give you difficulty, as identified by the type of person who
displays each pattern: the attacker, the sniper, the know-it-all,
the overcommiter, the indecisive, the whiner, the despairer,
and the zipper mouth.

Patterns of Difficult Behavior Identified by Personality Type

The *attacker* is called a "Sherman Tank" by Robert M.
Bramson.[1] Attackers are abusive and intimidating. They tend
to see others as inferior, so they have a right to run over them.
They view others as nobodies. Attackers feel they have a right
to tell people what they should do. They expect others to be
intimidated by them because, after all, they are superior.

Learning to deal with a person with this type of difficult
behavior requires you to develop the ability to stand up for
yourself. The attacker will continue to abuse and intimidate
you if you acquiesce or remain passive or non-assertive. Even
though the attacker sees you as an inferior human being,
remember that no one can make you feel inferior without your
permission. As a young, inexperienced social services worker
in child welfare in rural Alabama, I encountered an attacker
who was my supervisor. She was large in body build; had broad
shoulders and a deep, gruff voice; and intimidated me by her
walk and overpowering presence. I could hear her walking
down the hall barking orders, and I quivered, wondering as a
novice social worker whether I had made a mistake in my case
entry or my intake procedure. I never stood up to her, and I
obeyed her implicitly, never questioning her recommenda-
tions or instructions. In retrospect, I realize that I allowed her
to intimidate me because of my own insecurity.

The *sniper* is skilled in sarcasm and humor.[2] I characterize this behavior as "digging" behavior. The sniper makes comments that "hit below the belt," and the blow is felt in the stomach. Snipers often aim for one particular person in a group. Rick Brinkman and Rick Kirschner describe the sniper thusly: "Whether through rude comments, biting sarcasm, or a well-timed roll of the eyes, making you look foolish is the sniper's specialty."[3]

In dealing successfully with snipers, the goal is to bring them out of hiding—"blow their cover." Ask them what they are really trying to say.[4] Most snipers I know will respond with one of two comments. Number one is, "Can't you take a joke?" The second is, "You're just too sensitive." Once you have confronted a sniper, he or she usually will cease the sniping behavior with you.

Sometimes you will find a sniper in a Sunday school class or church. You may think you are leading a powerful discussion, and the sniper, usually from the back of the room, will pour "cold water" on your presentation, raise a question about your credibility or preparation, or seek to get the attention of the group. Other times a sniper will make a snide remark about your appearance, your weight, or your apparel. I found that confrontation is very effective in dealing with snipers. Convey to them that your preference is open and honest communication.[5]

I once knew a sniper in a professional relationship who habitually poked fun at my clothing, implying in a group that I was attempting to influence others with my choice of colors. The insinuations implied or interpreted by me were not complimentary. In fact, they were often disgusting. I felt that confrontation was necessary, and the result was that the sniping stopped, and the sniper became a friend and supportive colleague.

Another type of person who displays difficult behavior is the *expert* or know-it-all. Experts feel they have every right to make all the decisions and to tell others what to do because they are usually knowledgeable and competent people. They have predetermined that their way is best.[6] They actually feel called of

God to try to run other people's lives, to dominate, and perhaps to manipulate and control.

In relating successfully to experts, do not try to know more than they do, but be prepared to present your ideas briefly or indirectly. You may eventually win their respect.[7]

I met an expert as a school social worker when I first moved to New Orleans. She was perhaps the best social worker I have ever known, and she knew a great deal cognitively and experientially. She had worked in the city system for twenty years when I arrived from rural Alabama. She was my supervisor, and a good one. We had a supervision meeting once weekly, and I always quivered in my boots before entering her office. She could find the most minute details and inquire about the "whys" and "wherefores" of my decisions or lack of decisions.

One day as she was examining my records she noted that I had not received a response to a request I had made from an agency three weeks earlier. She pounced on me with questions: How did I let this happen? Why had I not called or written again? As a final reprimand she asked, "Don't you have a car? Don't you know you can drive across town and retrieve the form?" I did know that, but I actually thought that her suggestion was not really the best plan. Did I say that to my supervisor? Absolutely not. I was too scared that she would scream at me before the entire staff, and I would be intimidated and embarrassed.

But I would like to have another try at that experience. I would screw my courage to the sticking point, look her in the eye, and say, "You may be right, and I'll do what you as my supervisor tell me, but I really don't think that is the best plan. I'd like to be more patient, investigate further, and give the agency more time to respond. But if you tell me to go, I will." She might have listened had I been courageous. After all, I wasn't dumb—I did have a good record with her. Oh, for chances missed to learn about handling difficult behavior! Part of our thinking usually is that the behavior will go away if we ignore it, but it never does. The one staff member who was assertive with this supervisor did gain her respect.

You will meet some *overcommiters* in the church. Brinkman and Kirschner label these difficult people as "Yes Persons."[8] They are very likable people and say yes to any request, but they overcommit, and their follow-through leaves much to be desired. Because these people want to be liked, they make unrealistic agreements. Bramson identifies such persons as super-agreeable and thinks that they are hard to work or deal with because they cannot be counted on.[9]

My experience has been that I may have to protect overcommiters from themselves, help them set limits to their commitments, and often be willing to compromise. I have a cousin who is very special to me, but I have allowed her to drive me up the wall when we try to plan family get-togethers for holidays. I will invite her for lunch, and she will commit to a 1:00 P.M. time. I'm usually ready at one, food on the table, hungry, and no guest. About two she will call—she has been detained, and she always has a very legitimate excuse: flat tire, lost something, had an emergency toothache, you name it. She'll be there by three. I wait until three, getting angrier by the minute. By four she may arrive—laughing, amused, and explaining. I'm frustrated, resentful, and vowing I'll never invite her again. But she is enjoyable company, and I probably will make allowances for her again. Over the years I have learned to compromise by suggesting we have holiday dinners late. That way my individual family can eat at noon when we choose. She is happier because she can sleep late and drive the distance when the mood strikes her. We both like it better since we have decided to compromise.

Indecisive persons also can be very frustrating to deal with in personal as well as professional relationships. According to Bramson, "Decisions are emotional experiences for them because they want to please everyone; therefore they stall."[10] In dealing with a staller, it may be helpful to make it easy for him to be direct and specific. Ask questions, help him problem solve, and examine facts. Another helpful technique may be to come up with a decisive plan, or perhaps to try rank-ordering alternatives.[11]

Stallers really do bother me personally. I feel that I can deal with any situation as long as I receive direct, accurate, and concise information; but to handle wishy-washiness is frustrating to me. Often in a group, individuals will have difficulty deciding where to go to eat, what to order, or what time to go. I find I want to help them make a decision.

Whiners display another type of difficult behavior that you will observe in every group, church included. Whiners often are called complainers, and they gripe about everything.[12] Some complainers are very skilled in this habit. They have practiced well and have had an abundance of experience. They see themselves as powerless and consider themselves victims. They feel they have no control over their situations. I often have wondered whether some persons were born with more whining genes than others. Whiners often do not know what they want; they just seem to want to complain.

You'll meet whiners in every congregation. I know several. You know how Baptists are prone to sit in the same pew every Sunday. My husband and I are in this rut too, and there is a whiner who sits two pews behind us. She habitually gripes about the temperature in the sanctuary. The church is either too hot or too cold, and she declares she is going home if somebody doesn't do something about it. I don't think she knows what she wants done; I think she just wants attention. I find it very tempting to say to her, "Why don't you just go?" I often do offer her my coat or jacket.

Bramson points out that in order to cope with this type of behavior, we need to listen attentively and acknowledge what the whiners have to say. He also advises us not to agree, but to try to problem solve.[13]

Despairers are those who see the dark side of every situation. They are naysayers. Bramson refers to these troublesome characters as "negatives" or "wet blankets." They throw cold water on every suggestion or idea presented and can name immediately many reasons why an idea won't work.[14] Negatives in the church will point out to you that "we've tried that idea, and it didn't work." These persons are definitely not my favorite people to be around. They do seem to sap energy, and continued contact with gloomy persons will affect your attitude if you are not cautious and fight against the tendency to be pulled down into despair.

My tendency is to avoid negative people because their presence tends to drain me. My experience has been that negative people can spoil plans or dampen them if I allow it to happen.[15] I encounter despairers when I suggest we go to Cafe Du Monde in the French Quarter for beignets (donuts) and coffee at night. Often a gloomy friend will object by saying something like, "No, no, don't do that. Didn't you hear that someone was killed near there last week?" "Well, yeah, but someone was also killed on Gentilly Boulevard not far from my home last week," I say. "And besides, we all have to go some time, so we might as well have beignets and coffee on the way out."

While planning a mission trip to Australia, I encountered numerous persons who opposed the idea. Some comments were, "Don't you know that trip requires eighteen hours of flying? All kinds of tragedies can happen in eighteen hours. Why don't you pick a country closer by? Studying social work in another country won't help your own students." I found that I am most successful dealing with a "no" person if I accept his viewpoint, acknowledge that he may be right, but go anyway.[16] You can't allow a despairer to spoil your plans or your life. Maintain your positive attitude.

Another type of person with difficult behavior you may encounter at home, especially if you have a teenager in your family, is the *zipper mouth*. This person controls by silence. He answers questions with a yes or no and offers no comments. Bramson identifies these persons as "clams."[17] All of us know there is power in silence because most of us are uncomfortable with silence. In dealing with a silent type, I have found it helpful to be direct and state my expectations. You cannot allow such a person to control through silence and a refusal to respond. If you are in charge, you really do have to take control and state expectations and possible consequences.

Perspectives on Difficult Behavior

According to Paul Meier, the world is full of jerks, people who are selfish and filled with entitlement and an attitude of "I deserve to act, be, or have what I want."[18] He also reminds us that a part of each one of us is a "jerk" too.[19]

Once we have examined ourselves to see how, when, and to whom we are difficult, we can resolve to do something about our behavior. We are not victims; we can change. We can read the Bible and ask God to search our heart and see if there is any wickedness within us.[20]

Keep in mind that we cannot change others; we can only change our behavior and attitude toward them. We can depersonalize their behavior, and understanding may give us more tolerance of them. Learning to be assertive and to confront difficult behavior is a process, and the ability to cope can be developed.[21] We need to learn to confront as constructively and caringly as possible. I have a spiritual mentor, C. Ferris Jordan, who advises that when he encounters people with difficult behavior, he asks two questions: "Why has God sent these people into my life?" and "What can I learn from them?" I personally have not reached this level of spiritual maturity yet, but I think these questions are excellent to promote spiritual growth. I believe that behind every difficult behavior there is a hurt, and I need to attempt to understand that everyone may not be as blessed as I have been. God has blessed me with loving parents; concerned extended family; a devoted spouse; faithful friends; affirming students; and a meaningful, fulfilling profession. How grateful I am!

CHAPTER 16

Building a Culture for Managing Church Conflict

Steve Echols

The Goal of Healthy Churches

Recently a denominational employee was lamenting the large number of Southern Baptist churches in his state that were in serious conflict. He noted that though he had no scientific polling to prove it, nonetheless, he believed that one-third had a level of conflict that would be at least a three on the five-point scale of church conflict developed by Speed Leas. Few who have been among a large number of Southern Baptist churches would doubt this observation. The Leas scale has become the one to which most Southern Baptist church-minister relations specialists refer. His scale includes five levels: Level one—Problems to be solved, Level two—Disagreements, Level three—Contests, Level four—Fight/Flight, Level five—Intractable solutions.[1]

That so many churches could have reached the level in which problems have become contests is disturbing indeed. No wonder such a large percentage of churches are in plateau or are on the decline. Conflict drains energy and resources away from the primary mission of the church. Yet, because there are always problems to be solved, conflict happens. This is not a news flash. The question is whether we can keep problems from escalating into contests, which inevitably become personal and result in severe damage to the unity and ultimately to the mission of the church. The answer is yes. We can, because Jesus has empowered us to do so.

On the eve of His crucifixion, Jesus prayed the high priestly prayer in which He petitioned God for His followers in a number of areas. One of the petitions that He made for His followers was that they grow in unity.[2] This is a sacred unity in that it is patterned after the unity of the Father and Son.[3] The good news of reconciliation must be modeled by any church that exemplifies such in its relationships among its members. What Jesus proposed was not the norm for human nature and was not even the norm for the relationships among His disciples. What Jesus petitioned for was a radically different type of culture, a culture of the Kingdom.

A number of qualities can be identified in a church that has a healthy culture for dealing with problems. Among these are the five mentioned in this article. When these qualities are in place, it does not mean that there are no problems. Nor does it mean that there is no dissatisfaction. However, the key is that instead of destructive dissatisfaction and strife, creative energy can be exerted to work through the difficulties. Working through the process actually becomes an opportunity for the maturing of the body in working toward the goal of growing in unity.

Building the Culture through Integrity

Reporting their results from extensive surveys in regard to the qualities that followers most desired to see in their leaders, James Kouzes and Barry Posner noted that the number one quality was honesty. This quality ranked well ahead of other desired traits such as forward looking, inspiring, or competent. They added that people will follow a person into situations, no matter how dangerous, if he or she is trustworthy. "They want to know that the would-be leader is truthful and ethical."[4] This trust factor is critically important when problems arise and differences emerge.

How is trust built? Step by step, moment by moment, trust is built in little ways that add up. Years ago, I was in a church that desperately needed to construct a new children's building. The potential for conflict was great. Initially, most of the people in the church wanted either a new auditorium or a family life center. A planning committee had done a detailed study and concluded that the next step should be a children's building. Personally, I would have loved to have had a new auditorium or family life center. Yet, neither of these would really have been what the church needed the most. The passions ran deep on the issue. Clearly, things had progressed beyond a problem to be solved and had reached level two on the Leas scale, a disagreement.

One deacons' meeting was particularly critical. The decisive ingredient that swayed the moment was the trust factor. In the end, the deacons and the congregation supported the committee overwhelmingly because it was made up of people they trusted. They had seen their integrity in many ways that may have seemed small but ultimately added up when the big moment came. The trust factor is the difference between bringing down a conflict from a level two to a level one (a problem to be solved) rather than going up to a level three (a contest).

A practical and essential principle for building integrity is simply to do what is promised. This is especially critical for ministers. Seemingly little things such as providing supplies for a teacher or making a visit can build trust. The key is that every promise that a minister makes is seen as a test of his or her integrity. Therefore, promises should not be made flippantly. When a commitment is made, careful notes should be taken so as to insure follow-up. People are observing to see if it will be done, and it will make a critical difference in creating a healthy culture for managing church conflict.

Building the Culture through Vision

The writer of Proverbs declared the value of a vision: "Where there is no vision, the people perish."[5] The Hebrew word translated *vision* here means "a divine revelation."[6] The implication is that a vision involves a word from the Lord. The church can only be unified by a word from the Lord, a vision for His purposes.

I have had the wonderful privilege of serving as a pastor for nearly twenty-five years. In every church I have served, the congregation was either on the plateau or in decline when I became the pastor. I count it a great blessing to have been part of a team effort that in each case was able to see the church turn around and begin to grow again.

Students often ask about the primary factor that made the difference. I respond that first and foremost a leadership team must have total integrity as evidenced under the Lordship of Christ. Once that commitment is made, the number one factor for turning churches around is renewed vision. However, renewed vision does more than help a church grow again. It creates a healthy culture for managing church conflict. In fact, both of these aspects are closely related.

Conflict can sometimes emerge from a growing dissatisfaction from an individual or group in regard to some issue. Yet, this situation does not have to be negative but depends on whether the dissatisfaction is constructive or destructive in nature. Examples of destructive dissatisfaction abound in the typical complaints about issues and individuals in the church. Much energy is often expended in putting out these fires. On the other hand, constructive dissatisfaction does not seek to be critical, but helpful. The intention is not to attack, but to reconcile, not to exacerbate the problem, but to help find solutions to it. The difference is huge, and the role of vision is the critical difference between the two.

In a church that has caught a common vision (and that vision should be of course a word from God), a great challenge is accepted. This challenge is one that calls the church as a whole to repentance, humility, and sacrificial service for the greater Kingdom cause. When this type of response occurs, there is neither the time nor the inclination to lay blame. Resources are viewed as too precious to waste on petty conflict. A significant measure of how well the vision has been embraced is evidenced by whether there is full employment of the congregation in ministries that are spawned by the vision. Marshall Shelley noted that the more church members were fully employed in ministries, the less likely they were to become sources of strife and disunity.[7] In the case of preventing the escalation of conflict, it is true that an idle hand in regard to ministry is the devil's workshop.

When a vision is cast and accepted, alignment occurs, supernatural synergism develops, and the church far exceeds what it was previously doing in terms of Kingdom work. When energy flows toward the vision, there is less energy available for issues that are destructive. There develops a strong cultural admonition against it. It is very much like when a nation is at war. A natural unity flows out of the sense of urgency for the vision. Problems to solve or even disagreements to resolve will never disappear. However, they are less likely to get to the level three of contests, which can cripple the unity of the church.

Building the Culture through the Modeling of Leaders

Followers get their cues from leaders. In churches, it is vitally important that the leadership develop and model a healthy culture for handling conflict. Otherwise, the congregation will not. The church staff is of particular importance. I have seldom known a church with a multi-staff to have serious unity problems if the church staff members were functioning well as a team. Such churches just naturally seem to know how to keep issues at a level of being only problems to solve. Even if opinions evolve into formal disagreements, it is more difficult to find lay members who have the influence to move the conflict to the contest stage. When it does occur, the influence of a united staff can do much to bring the conflict down to a more manageable level.

On the other hand, where the staff is divided, almost inevitably the church will be divided as well. Ministry pitted against ministry and personality against personality draws others into the fray. Staff terminations are particularly destructive. W. A. Criswell observed that the termination of a staff minister involves others in the congregation. He added, "I have never gone through it, but that we have not lost families from the church, no matter how unworthy the staff worker."[8]

The influence that staff members have by virtue of their positions makes their working together in harmony essential. Likewise, the staff does not simply need to model unity among themselves but also with all of the leaders in the church. The influence can be similar to that of parents who model healthy relationships and the positive effect they can have on their children.

Building the Culture through Intentional Process

Change is stressful, and churches face plenty of it. Despite the common misperception that some churches never change, churches are living organisms that are in constant evolvement. Congregation members age, move, and die while new members join. The community changes rapidly or slowly, but it always changes. Change stresses organisms, and the church is no exception. As a result, conflict may come. Dealing with the fallout as problems to be solved rather than contests to be won, is one of the greatest challenges that leaders face. Jesus said that men do not put new wine into old wineskins lest the wineskins burst. Rather the new wine must be put into new wineskins so that both are preserved.[9] Church leaders must bring new wineskins of new structure to hold the reality of the new wine of change.

A simple three-step process can help build consensus when challenges come. First, in every change setting there must be an initiating group. These are the people who are out front in seeing the reality and the opportunity of the changes that are occurring. Every idea has to start somewhere, but the more people involved the better. The writer of Proverbs stated, "In the multitude of counsellors there is safety."[10]

There is no set formula to determine who should be part of the initiating group. Often, however, it does not follow the lines of formal committee structure, but rather is an informal ad hoc group. Who should be involved will vary from issue to issue. Good leaders are able to discern who should be consulted on the front end of an idea. Likewise, the number of individuals who are part of the initiating group will vary. Usually, however, the number will be relatively small.

The second step in the process of change strategy is the formal legitimizing of the idea. Formal bodies such as committees and deacons are critical, but the opinion leaders who do not hold formal positions may be just as important. If change proposals are implemented without legitimization, serious conflict is almost inevitable. This part of the process takes time, but the rewards are well worth the effort. Even if total unanimity is not achieved, serious resistance can be defused.

The third step is the building of a consensus. In traditional Southern Baptist polity, the local church is the final authority. Yet, whether matters are voted on is not the primary issue. The small number of people who may attend a Wednesday night business meeting does not insure that the matter has a consensus. The careful leader works hard to make certain that as many of the congregation as possible have been informed and have bought into the change. Obviously, the magnitude of the decision determines whether a full mobilization is necessary. Yet, if an issue has the potential of being a source of major conflict, then every effort should be made to build an overwhelming consensus before implementation.

How is a consensus built? A careful and passionate commitment to communication is the key. An often-repeated mistake is to rely on less personal means of communication such as church bulletins, e-mails, letters, or general announcements. Though the redundancy of these channels can be of great reinforcement, they are much less effective than face-to-face communication in individual or small group settings. How can one be sure if communication has actually occurred? The only way is to receive feedback. In a non-ego-threatening fashion, the communicator must solicit a response to see if the idea has gotten across. Something like the following might be said: "I have proposed a lot today. Tell me how you see all of this playing out." Such an invitation should elicit a response that will enable the proponent to hear how well he or she has communicated.

A practical example of how the process works comes from an experience at my last pastorate before I joined the seminary faculty. We were involved in a strategic plan called Vision 2000.

A number of goals had been set that included a large amount of new construction and renovation. In a special moment of prayer time, I felt very strongly that God was leading us to give a mission tithe (ten percent of our receipts to mission causes) from all the funds that we would receive for our capital projects.

Although I felt strongly that it was the right thing to do, I did not just announce it to the church or even to any formal leadership group. Instead, I asked several trusted leaders from different segments of the church to pray with me about it and to let me know how they felt God was speaking to them about this idea. After praying about it, each one affirmed that they felt convinced that God was leading us to give a mission tithe. Next, we went to the formal legitimizing bodies such as the deacons and other key committees.

Along the way, we carefully informed other stakeholders. We were so intentional and deliberate in the communication process that the support was overwhelming. When the opportunity to start two new church plants, which involved sending out two of the church staff with massive support, was later proposed, the support remained strong. The result was the natural outcome of the decision that had already been made. Opposition and conflict were held to an absolute minimum, and later the church had a cause for rejoicing at the success of the new churches. Going through the process took time, but the time saved in not having to deal with potentially divisive conflict was even greater.

Building the Culture through a Willingness to Confront in Love

Level one of the Leas scale is the presence of a problem to be solved. Confronting problems is not pleasant, but the willingness to do so provides a leadership opportunity. John Maxwell observed that people generally do not want to deal with problems at all. Consequently, they will put "the reins of leadership into your hands—if you are willing to and able to either tackle their problems or train them to solve them."[11]

The TV character Barney Fife on the *Andy Griffith Show* often used to say, "You've got to nip it in the bud . . . nip it, nip it, nip it!" There is much to be gained in the "nip it" philosophy when attempting to build a culture to manage conflict. Problems to be solved are much less formidable than contests to be won. Jesus communicated the same urgency in dealing with conflict when He instructed that one should even leave in the middle of an act of worship to deal with a problem with a brother.[12]

To deal with an issue quickly does not guarantee de-escalation. More important, the manner in which the Scripture instructs us to deal with conflicts is critical. Jesus exhorted His followers to love their enemies.[13] In other words, Christians were to avoid bitter contests. They were to deal with issues with integrity, refusing to compromise on what is right. Yet, by turning the other cheek, there would be an opportunity to defuse the conflict much in the same way that the writer of Proverbs noted that "a soft answer turneth away wrath."[14] This approach corresponds with Paul's admonition about "speaking the truth in love."[15] Christians who love one another care enough to confront. They know that problems do not go away by themselves. By building a culture in which members are not afraid to address problems in a loving manner, spiritual leaders help foster the unity for which Jesus prayed on the eve of His crucifixion.

CHAPTER 17

Relating to the Church Staff

Jerry N. Barlow

And they, continuing daily with one accord in the temple . . . .

Acts 2:46

Staff relationships should be exemplary Christian relationships. That is, pastors and staff members must build the kind of interpersonal relationships that can serve as examples of what Christ desires relationally within a church family and between believers and others. Good Christian relationships between pastors and staff members will also facilitate their work and the work of the church. How can pastors and staff members build such relationships?

Two factors are of prime importance in good staff relationships. Those factors are climate and cooperation. The pastor must take responsibility for establishing the right kind of climate for building good staff relationships. Likewise, staff members must take responsibility for establishing good relationships with the pastor through cooperation. Staff must also cooperate well with each other. How can all of this happen?

The Right Kind of Climate

Pastors and staff members do not serve together in a vacuum, but in an organizational environment that either helps or hinders their relationships and work. Thus, the climate of a church is a set of conditions that affect how pastors and staff

175

members communicate, make decisions, feel motivated, handle conflict, work as a team, and show concern for each other. The right kind of climate can contribute to good staff relationships by facilitating communication between pastors and staff members, as well as within the staff. Such a climate empowers decision making, nurtures the best effort, smoothes out problems and disagreements, fosters a team spirit, and develops loyalty and love. But what conditions produce such a positive climate?

One key condition is openness. Pastors can establish a climate of openness by keeping staff members informed, being receptive to their ideas and suggestions, soliciting their evaluative feedback, and encouraging staff members to do the same with each other. Sometimes, perhaps because of ego or insecurity, pastors may exclude staff members from strategic planning with church leaders and from the communication loop in other matters. Such actions can create a climate of resentment and hurt. Without the pastor's leadership, staff members can do the same to each other.

Another important condition is trust. Trust occurs when a person comes to believe in the integrity and reliability of another person. A pastor can foster trust when staff members observe and experience honesty in pastor-staff interpersonal interactions, causing staff members to develop confidence and closeness with the pastor. However, self-centered and un-Christlike behavior can cause a lack of trust and can even damage relationships between pastors and staff members or among staff.

A third condition significant for building the right kind of climate involves recognition and appreciation. Staff members often labor behind the scenes, while pastors are more noticed, especially when churches achieve growth in membership and ministries. Pastors build and encourage good relationships with staff members and among staff members by "giving credit where credit is due." But pastors who feel threatened by, or are jealous of, the giftedness of staff members may take personal credit for the work and accomplishments of staff, leaving staff members feeling unappreciated and perhaps angry. Such a climate does not build good pastor-staff relationships.

Christians should forgive one another and seek forgiveness. The right kind of staff climate depends upon the practice and condition of giving and seeking forgiveness. Neither pastors nor staff members are perfect in character, conduct, and conversation. While personal perspective and ego may affect how one sees who is at fault and who is right or wrong, pastors must show through Christian humility that people and relationships are more important than winning an argument or placing blame. Failing to forgive or seek forgiveness dishonors Christ and divides relationships. As the recognized leader and example for all, a pastor should take the first step in forgiving "as Christ forgave" (Col. 3:13) or in going to a staff member "who hath ought against" the pastor (Matt. 5:23-24).

However, none of the previous conditions will come to exist unless pastors take a genuine interest in staff members and show loving actions toward them. Sometimes staff members see pastors as being interested only in themselves and their career path. Pastors who sincerely shepherd and befriend staff members help staff to feel needed and not to feel used. Out of such a climate, pastors and staff members can build relationships of respect and admiration—relationships that can last a lifetime!

Cooperation

Cooperation means working together. Certainly, staff members should work well with the pastor and with each other. However, Christian cooperation involves more than actions—it also includes attitudes. Sometimes staff members carry out their responsibilities and tasks in an uncooperative spirit toward the pastor or other staff. Such an attitude makes it hard for staff to enjoy their work, give their best, and build good relationships with pastors and other staff ministers. What can be done to nurture cooperation, a good attitude toward others, and the building of relationships?

Shared goals help to improve cooperation, attitude, and relationships. All Christians and Christian churches have responsibility for carrying out the Great Commission of Christ,[1] and staff members should take responsibility for their personal part in that undertaking. But they also bear a responsibility for leading others in their program or ministry area to act in accomplishing the Great Commission. By sharing personally and organizationally in this overall goal, staff members can build a bridge in relationship with the pastor and other staff. In effect, team building and better relationships will develop as everyone "pulls on the same rope."

However, other goals are not always shared and may even cause conflict. For example, a pastor may emphasize evangelism with little emphasis on discipleship, causing a staff member in discipleship grave concern. Another staff member may desire priority for facility use or budget allotment to the detriment of program areas overseen by other staff. Staff members so affected must take responsibility for their reactions and actions in response. They must strive to communicate their concerns and opinions with Christian grace.[2] The Golden Rule should be the rule that guides their responses and decisions.[3] In these ways, staff members can keep different goals and exclusive aims from diminishing their relationship with the pastor or other staff. Often, a spirit of teamwork will result— and stronger relationships also.

The same is true for shared perspective. Relationships depend upon a common perspective about numerous matters. But people do not always see things the same way. Unfortunately, differences in perspectives of pastors and staff members can adversely affect cooperation and relationships.

While pastors bear much responsibility for communicating how they see things, staff members have a responsibility for being willing to listen and to strive to understand the pastor's perspective. Sometimes generational differences affect how pastors and staff members see things (and how willing they are to listen and try to understand each other). Levels and types of experience also can affect perspective and understanding, as can upbringing and personality. By identifying the possible factors affecting a difference in perspective, staff members can react with Christian respect and tolerance toward an older or younger pastor. Such a reaction and attitude may even serve as the catalyst for improved cooperation and relationships.

Joint problem solving often fosters cooperation and better relationships. Whether the problem needing to be solved is organizational or relational, pastor-staff relationships can grow closer in the process of resolving the problem satisfactorily. However, they can grow colder in relationship too, if the problem is not resolved or not resolved satisfactorily. To keep relationships from deteriorating under the stress of problems, staff members should keep their focus on problem issues and not on personality issues (such as ego, for example). They also should not enlarge the complexity of the problem by bringing in others as supporters, instead of as resources to resolve the problem. While staff members compose only one part of a joint problem-solving process, that part can be instrumental in determining how the other party participates and in how the problem is solved. Just as Paul and John Mark grew closer after their mission trip problem,[4] so pastors and staff members can grow closer as they journey together down the road of life's problems.

Feedback and Self-Disclosure

While climate and cooperation aid the building of good interpersonal relationships, so do feedback and self-disclosure between pastors and staff members, as well as staff members with each other. People can learn about one another through the interpersonal processes of giving feedback and providing self-disclosure. How do these processes work?

One simple explanation of the processes of feedback and self-disclosure in interpersonal relationship building comes from the Johari Window. The Johari Window, originally proposed by psychologists Joseph Luft and Harry Ingham to aid group process (its name is a combination of "Joseph" and

"Harry"), represents a picture of self in interpersonal interaction with other persons.[5] Using this instrument, ministers can evaluate themselves through each of four relational windows and assess their strengths and weakness regarding self-disclosure.

Through whatever process we use, we can count on God to help us as we develop pastor-staff relationships through feedback and disclosure. For example, while God sometimes directly helps a person to learn about himself, as He did with Moses,[6] the Lord often uses others to expand one's self-awareness, as He did with David through Samuel,[7] Saul through Ananias,[8] and Timothy through Paul.[9] For this reason, pastors and staff members need to grow in their relationship with Christ, so that the Lord can use them as encouragers of each other with insights about themselves and one another as guided by the Holy Spirit.

Feedback from others can be painful. Also, self-disclosure is not always easy and requires both risk and trust. Yet, the potential payoff can be the building of edifying, enriching, Christ-honoring relationships. And, remember—this is what Jesus invited when He said, "And learn from Me, for I am meek and lowly of heart" (Matt. 11:29).

The Example for Pastor-Staff Relationships

For pastor-staff relationships to be exemplary Christian relationships, pastors and staff members should follow the example of Jesus toward the disciples. Jesus loved, taught, advised, counseled, comforted, and empowered His disciples. He also served as a model for them in humility, concern, faithfulness, patience, and openness. He called them His friends[10] and considered them to be family.[11] The best pastor-staff relationships are like that.

As pastors and staff members serve the Lord together, their relationships should grow into deep friendship with a love for one another as family. When pastors set the right kind of climate, and staff members work together with the pastor and with each other, their relationships grow to be all that human relationships can be, even despite great difficulties and demands in life and ministry. What a blessing it is to honor Christ by building strong interpersonal relationships![12]

Relationship Assessment Exercise

Please complete the following statements that pertain to your *current* church staff position by circling the number that *best* reflects your situation *now.* After you have done so, assess your pastor-staff relationship(s) by identifying relationship strengths to maintain and any areas of needed improvement in the relationship(s). As a result of your assessment, you may find it helpful to review this chapter and consult the books suggested for further reading (see the Recommended Reading section at the back of this book).

A. Relationship Assessment for Pastors

1. My relationship with staff members now is_____.
    1. not good   2. good   3. very good

2. My relationship with staff members now _____.
    1. is not improving   2. is improving some   3. does not
                                               need improving

3. My relationship with staff members now is best characterized by _____.
    1. openness   2. trust   3. giving and
                                         seeking forgiveness
    4. genuine interest in them   5. all of these

4. Staff members cooperate with me _____.
    1. somewhat   2. mostly   3. fully

5. My relationship with staff members is like Jesus' relationship with the disciples_____.
    1. somewhat   2. mostly   3. fully

B. Relationship Assessment for Staff Members

1. My relationship with the pastor now is _____.
   1. not good   2. good   3. very good

2. My relationship with the pastor now _____.
   1. is not improving   2. is improving some   3. does not
                                               need improving

   3. My relationship with the pastor now is best characterized
by _____.
   1. openness   2. trust   3. giving and seeking forgiveness
   4. his genuine interest in me 5. all of these

   4. I cooperate with the pastor _____.
   1. somewhat   2. mostly   3. fully

   5. My relationship with the pastor is like Jesus' relationship
with the disciples _____.
   1. somewhat   2. mostly   3. fully

CHAPTER 18

Relationships at Church:
A Testimony

Fred and Elizabeth Luter

Our united relationship with Jesus Christ has many branches. The branches have extended farther than we could imagine. One special branch has reached into the depth of the congregation where it has created a unique relationship. There is a kindred spirit between the pastoral family and the members. This bond cannot be easily explained. Where there isn't a solid relationship in the home, the pastor-parishioner relationship can be staggering. When the Godhead has free rein with the shepherd and his spouse, solidarity can exist. When the equilibrium is off balance, the body suffers for attention.

A special friend attended two of our church services and one off-site church outing. She observed a unique blend of fellowship among us. "The people appear to respect both of you," she stated. "It is not just the positions of pastor and wife. They're not patronizing you, but they're freely interacting."

As pastor, my favorite quote is, "If you get the head right, the body will follow." There must be a well-balanced relationship between the leader and the Godhead. It can create an environment conducive to genuine church and family relationships.

In a growing church, there is always a struggle to maintain harmony. Rapid growth presents an even greater problem. A healthy relationship with and within the increasing congregation is necessary. When protocol is established, there is less confusion for everyone involved, including new members who are able to determine quickly whether the church is a place where they can function.

As a family, we have discovered a tremendous need for flexibility. Life is always changing, and so are relationships. While some members will move closer in meaningful relationship, many will distance themselves. The shifting of positions will allow everyone to become a part of the body. This knowledge can eliminate the hard task of cultivating and maintaining original relationships.

As many new support ministries are added, the responsibility to maintain relationships will change as other leaders exemplify the vision. When the hearts and visions of leaders are not the same as the pastor's, disharmony develops immediately. The best decision for us has been to move slowly and allow God to work things out. Time will expose a leader's separate agenda. Then the hidden agenda is revealed to a larger audience. The whole body benefits from the lesson that is learned.

In the beginning of our ministry, the church consisted of only sixty-five members. I started a practice of calling out the members' names during the sermon, which proved beneficial in remembering their names. The incorporation of the new members' class was an additional gem. The weekly one-hour sessions lasted for four weeks. When the pastor teaches the new members' class, new names can be added to the memory as the roll is called. While teaching the new members lessons, the process of calling their names formed new bonds. Each Sunday at the end of a session, everyone repeated his or her name. The names that were most memorable were added to the memory bank and later called out in the sermons. The relationships grew as many proclaimed, "Pastor knows my name."

Today, growth of the church to more than six thousand members makes the process of name calling quite challenging. As the memory wanes, I am limited to utilizing the names of those with the earliest bonds. This practice has sharpened old relationships.

To generate and cultivate new relationships, we frequently attend different ministry functions. We arrive early enough to introduce ourselves and mingle throughout the crowd. At intermissions and closings we continue to mingle. We stay until we have touched everyone present in some way.

We challenge new members to get involved in a smaller circle of the ministry. When we just had Sunday school and one worship service a week, there were various fellowship times. At the beginning of each service, members were encouraged to fellowship for a brief moment. They would go throughout the congregation hugging and shaking hands. At the close of each service, fellowship continued in the hallways and parking lots. We were always the last ones to leave. When the members became better acquainted with each other, it became less important to have a close relationship with us. This development provided us the opportunity to foster new relationships.

Now that we have three Sunday morning services, there is little time for fellowship. The new extended arm is the counseling and support team. This team calls and nurtures new members while they are taking their introductory classes. A new members fellowship is planned quarterly. At this event all pastors and ministry leaders are introduced. Then all the new members introduce themselves. Many share a testimony of why they have chosen this particular fellowship. More than 50 percent of the comments include a reference to the bonds noticed between the pastor and the members. Other comments include a reference to the warmth received by the church body as a whole.

We would like to be able to proclaim that we are always warm and welcoming to visitors; in reality that is not so. The truth is that in this rapidly growing congregation, many cannot tell a member from a guest. This situation affords the blessed opportunity for all to be treated as family. With a large influx of new members, veteran members can sometimes feel the pain of the oldest child. The former attention from the pastor becomes more limited or no longer exists at all. This situation makes it necessary for us to show our support when we can. We make appearances at the celebrations and family concerns of our veteran members. Special priority is given to make sure they know that we are there in the crunch. The opportunities that have been presented have deepened our relationships.

Our senior ministry has been vital in keeping a stable church environment. Many of our seniors are rooted in the Word of God. They are independent and self-sufficient. They travel and participate in activities with other senior ministries across the country. Their Sunday school class is one of the largest in the church. Various age groups attend because of the seniors' zeal and enthusiasm. Instead of the young adults assisting the seniors, the seniors are providing for the young adults. They provide both spiritual nourishment and financial assistance. They have given clarity to the Titus relationships addressed by the apostle Paul.[1]

The seniors take a great load off of the pastor. They require the least of the pastor's time. They give the utmost respect to their middle-aged leader. The relationship is like that of a parent and a child. The seniors understand the burdens of the ministry. Many of them work hard to undergird the church. They put in long hours on Sundays and volunteer their time during the week. Although they are in the minority, they provide the majority of effort.

Their perseverance and independence allow more time for the shepherd to nurture the flock. They have properly assessed the church and discovered that many of the members are lambs. Our seniors display the true role of a mother and a father in the ministry. They receive the same respect that they give.

As pastor and wife, we have developed strong bonds with the men's and women's ministries, including both the music and teaching groups. The participants have a broad range of spiritual gifts. As we pour our lives into theirs, they are consistent in pouring their lives into others. They are not limited to a relationship with us. Neither are they content with just relating to one another. Their branches extend throughout the congregation. They are always looking for new and exciting ways to minister to the body.

Our biggest challenge has been to foster solid relationships with our children's and youth ministries. When we were younger, and the congregation was smaller, there was constant interaction with our youth. The children who grew up in the ministry were nurtured by parents and grandparents in their homes. Many church parents provided additional parenting for each child. We taught their Bible classes. Our children were in the same age groups, and many of them would "hang out" at our home. Our relationships were solid. Discipline was immediate because there was always a guardian around.

Then it became necessary to separate the children from the adults. Children's church replaced family worship, and the distance grew. We maintained some sense of relationship with the youth of our early years. This fact can be proven by their reactions toward us. Many have now completed high school. Several have entered or completed college within the last few years. They remember us well, and they never neglect to give us a big hug and a smile.

Then the church grew. Outreach extended to neighboring areas where there was very little parental support. Discipline became the main focus. Cries from the youth and children's pastors grew increasingly loud. Very few members of the church wanted to assist in what seemed like a hopeless situation. It appeared that we were only pouring water into broken vessels. Burnout of the support staff was immediate. Our participation was limited due to increasing demands in Sunday school and worship services. Although our appearances in children's and youth services were few and far between, we could see destruction from afar. The troubled youth and children were influencing those with great potential. Time spent disciplining replaced the time that was usually spent nurturing. There was very little evidence of fruitful lives.

Now we see a new ray of hope. We have a new surplus of parentally guided children. Discipline has risen to a new level in order to maintain the standards desired and expected. The change has created an environment conducive to teaching and learning. Now we have greater interaction in the hallways after services. Many of the children and youth will reach out for a hug.

As pastor, my heart aches when I must intervene in situations involving disgruntled members. I know that a wrong move or decision can negate all the years and energy used to build solid relationships. It is by far one of the worst situations to deal with in ministry. It ranks with the painful breakup of families, death, and news of adulterous relationships. Such problems keep me awake at night.

I have been the pastor of this congregation for more than fifteen years. For the past six years, my wife and I have prayed and intervened in more altercations than we could ever have imagined. We could understand if the struggles were between immature Christians or new members. The greatest dilemmas involve those with knowledge of and prolonged exposure to the Word of God. The worst scenario includes those who are or were best friends in the ministry. Major time is spent "putting out fires" in areas that appear safe. This situation limits the time available to give attention to those who are at greater risk. We recognize it as a well-planned scheme by the enemy to destroy God's church and program.

The struggle to maintain harmony and increase vibrant relationships has become more intense. But by the grace of God, through prayer and fasting, God still prevails. Solid relationships are on the rise. Hallelujah, glory to the Lamb!

In closing, we proclaim that there are no wasted relationships. Each relationship has its intended purpose in the church. Positive or negative interactions will cause clergy, as well as members, to grow closer to one another and to Christ. But for that to happen, we must ask for wisdom in every situation.

As a pastor, I am grateful that God has given me the ministry and the ability to promote reconciliation.[2] I refuse to allow anyone to be angry with me without offering that person an opportunity to make amends. I take great care in confronting members when I notice a change in their dispositions. I try to maintain an open attitude toward them. I have been blessed to greet and treat them continually with respect. I always extend an open and friendly handshake to all. By the grace of God, I have not sought retaliation by sermon or Bible lesson. This openness has allowed God the opportunity to rekindle relationships that could have been severed. His grace is sufficient.[3]

We genuinely love our congregation from the heart, and we believe that they genuinely love us. We are blessed beyond measure. We proclaim what Jesus stated in John 15:15 (paraphrased): "[We] call you not servants; for the servant knoweth not what his lord doeth; but [we] have called you friends; for all things that [we] have heard of [our] Father we have made known unto you."

We have been careful not to be dictators over God's people. We strive to minister from a servant perspective. We encourage the flock to serve God and the ministry only. This method has kept the shepherd from looking superior to the sheep. As a church, we are one body with many members.[4] And Jesus Christ is "the head of the body."[5]

PART V

Your Relationships in Your Community

CHAPTER 19

The Importance of Community Ministry and Interpersonal Relationships

Wallace T. Davis

Community ministry has to do with interpersonal relationships, and its success hinges on the ability to form meaningful relationships within the community. Community ministry should not be differentiated from church ministry. For the church, the community is where ministry takes place. Community ministry should not be seen as taking away from what occurs in the worship center or classroom, nor should it be seen as separate from worship and discipleship. Ministry is what takes place in real-life settings. It may occur in a church, in a hospital, or in the home of a poverty-stricken family. Ministry is about people, relating to them, and meeting their needs wherever they are found.

Outreach is a basic component of ministry. It is the church extending the pews into the community, tearing down the walls that separate the religious from the non-religious, from those of faith to those of little or no faith. Simply put, ministry is about meeting people where they are. It's "where the rubber meets the road" for the church. As blood is life to the body, so ministry is life to the church.

Too often, the church finds itself conflicted over a false dichotomy: whether to support ministry within the institution at the expense of ministry outside the walls of the church. It should be obvious that ministry to the church membership is valid and absolutely necessary, but the issue should never be *either/or*, but rather *both/and*. Community ministry mandates a balance between outreach and in-reach. Due to limited resources or a lack of vision, the church may find itself focusing ministerial activities on those who pay the bills and sustain the institution, or at least have the potential for being "good returns on the investment." In other words, homeless persons, welfare mothers, or AIDS patients are not likely to become major donors or be able to lend any material assistance to the church. The issue then is, who most *needs* the ministry of the church? The obvious answer is most often the person least likely to offer significant material support. As Jesus said in Matthew 9:12, "They that be whole need not a physician, but they that are sick." His call for ministry to "the least of these" (Matt. 25:40) and the servant role He modeled certainly should bear weight with those who profess to have a serious commitment to a biblical model of church ministry.

The early church had no walls, no institutional settings to support. It was involved in outreach—to the infirm, widows, and orphans. Deacons were established to serve those in need of daily bread and care. There was an accountability system; if able-bodied people did not work, they did not eat.[1] From a quick glance at these early models, it can be argued that civil government may not be the best vehicle for responding to people who, for whatever reason, cannot or will not care for themselves. The church, when functioning at its best, can be the ideal choice to meet community needs. Unparalleled in modern times, the current administration in Washington has called upon churches and faith-based groups to become significantly involved in responding to the needs of people in local communities. President George W. Bush has called it his "Faith-Based Initiative."

Requirements for Ministry

Some basic requirements are necessary in order to engage in ministry. Obviously, one cannot engage in Christian ministry without having a relationship with Jesus Christ and a spiritual depth to one's life. Beyond that, the basic requirements for effective ministry are leadership, vision, ethical and moral behavior, commitment, resources, and attitude.

Leadership is about removing barriers and empowering people. It is about encouraging and engaging people in ministry by uniquely using their gifts. Leadership is about service. Servant leadership, as Jesus Christ demonstrated, did not consist of some ceremonial show of waiting tables at a special dinner, but rather was seen in His lifestyle. Jesus, demonstrating a true servant heart, saw the needs of the down and out and responded to those needs. Church leadership that is self-serving contradicts the model presented by Jesus. When the primary motivation of church leadership consists of "What can we get out of it?" the servant role is abandoned. The issue must always be "What can we do for you? How may we meet your needs?" When the church assumes the servant role, it becomes the best vehicle to model God's redeeming love throughout the community it serves. It takes on a life of its own.

Even in the corporate world today, there is much talk about servant leadership. Robert K. Greenleaf developed this terminology after he spent thirty-eight years in a career at AT&T as vice president of management research. Since 1964, this concept has taken on a corporate value that is worth reviewing today, for many of those principles and values really are the same as those taught by Jesus Christ. Greenleaf has written much about the leader as servant. He maintains that all leadership should be through service.[2]

Vision is critical in providing effective ministry. Proverbs 29:18 offers, "Where there is no vision, the people perish." This biblical concept is as true today as it was then. Some persons look upon a crop when the field is "white already to harvest" (John 4:35) and say, "Where is the potential?" Others look upon the same field and see the present crop value, but they also see what it can be five years from now. Seeing potential—possibilities—is the beginning of a vision. One man decided not to accept the call to serve as pastor of a church because he saw no potential for growth. Another man accepted the church, and ten years later the church had grown to five times its former size. He saw the potential and gave himself to the task of ministry in that place. Ministry takes place when there is a vision, and often the vision grows as new possibilities occur.

Along with leadership and vision, there must also be ethical and moral behavior. Doing the right thing is imperative. Often, ethical behavior is compromised by conflicts of interest, which can rob ministers of their effectiveness. Leadership should be above reproach. Something seemingly as small as a pastor expecting others to buy his lunch may suggest that the man is primarily a taker and not a giver. A pastor and his wife contract with a builder to construct their new home. The contractor gives the pastor a really good deal . . . maybe to earn brownie points with God, maybe because of some guilt he feels this gesture will assuage. The pastor, fully aware of the contractor's misguided motive, still agrees to the inequitable deal. Another couple gives a young minister and his wife a new car, and they accept the gift. These images contradict servant leadership. There are already too many in our culture who see the church and its leadership as charities, with hands out to take, or worse yet, as leeches upon society.

Commitment is what keeps the ministry going when nothing else is working. Commitment is the difference between success and failure. Commitment has to do with not letting little things or big things interfere with achieving the desired outcome. Commitment has to do with perseverance, with "sticking with it" no matter what. Most effective ministries stay alive because of a determination that goes far beyond what is easy. Most ministries fail because someone quits. Winston Churchill passed along his formula for leading Britain successfully in the difficult days of WWII: "Never give in—never, never, never, never . . . give in except to convictions of honour and good sense." That's the kind of determination and commitment that ministry demands.

In some cases, even where a vision is created, resources are lacking. Often the "down and out" are overlooked in the community because of a lack of financial and human resources. Their situations call for an investment of resources of both time and money. They have little or nothing to offer. Consequently, they are often overlooked or avoided because they do not present a "good return on the investment." Tragically, even some megachurches, which have accumulated ample resources, continue to bypass opportunities to minister to the poor and disenfranchised because they are not seen as enhancing the "mega" model the church has embraced. Effective community ministry demonstrates an understanding of the value of human resources and is willing to invest whatever is necessary to meet the needs of people.

Probably nothing really matters as much as attitude. An attitude that devalues people on the basis of their ability to contribute, an attitude that categorizes persons on the basis of their relative value to the church, is an attitude that essentially denies the Gospel. An attitude that sees evangelism as separate from, or in opposition to, community ministry is an attitude that misunderstands the Gospel.

There are attitudes toward other people and attitudes toward ourselves. Both have the potential to interfere with effective ministry. An attitude that hurts outreach says "You don't count," "I can do it by myself," or "You don't fit the description of the kind of person I like." The Lone Ranger mentality just doesn't work. Too much independence and not enough interdependence will limit what can be done in effective ministry. An attitude can say "I know what's best" or "How can we find the best answers together?" Positive, healthy attitudes about people and ministry shaped by clear biblical models and imperatives will enable ministers to move mountains and reap harvests in the Kingdom enterprise.

Jesus as a Community Minister

How did Jesus spend His time as a minister? Was it predominately in the temple? In the synagogue? In the temple compound? The Gospels contain accounts of Jesus in the temple. On one occasion when Jesus visited the temple, He made a whip and used it as His point of mission.[3] On that occasion, He called attention to the materialistic values that detracted from the true purpose of the temple as a house of worship.[4] Some modern religious leaders have the approach backwards and would use the whip on those outside the church—the welfare mother, the alcoholic, the unwed mother. A church that is viewed as non-compassionate will never have an effective ministry.

In Luke 16:19-31, Jesus told a story about a certain rich man who "fared sumptuously every day" while "a certain beggar named Lazarus . . . was laid at his gate . . . desiring to be fed with the crumbs which fell from the rich man's table." The story was about a man who had ample opportunities to minister to one in need. It is the story about the wrong kind of relationship, an inadequate relationship between the rich and the poor. It identified a heart devoid of compassion. The rich man looked upon this beggar with leprosy lying at his door perhaps much as AIDS patients are viewed today. Those with leprosy represented a nuisance and evoked fear and mistrust. A relationship between the rich and poor never occurred.

Sometimes the church is afraid to reach out, fearing somehow that it will condone the acts of irresponsibility that got people into their current predicaments. Even then, many have not been able to differentiate between circumstances as a result of choice and circumstances not related to choice. Regardless of how they got there, hurting persons still need the compassion of the church. Reaching out is not about condoning, but about showing compassion.

While Jesus did spend some time in religious settings, it is obvious from the Gospel records that most of His time was spent moving among the people of the community.[5] He circulated among and spent time with tax collectors and other people of questionable reputations.[6] Children were drawn to Him, and He took time for them.[7] He engaged a Gentile woman in a well-side conversation.[8] He attended parties and socialized with everyday people in everyday situations.[9] Jesus was out among the people most of the time, and He remains forever the ultimate model of community ministry.

When Jesus and the disciples were on the Mount of

Transfiguration,[10] they had a powerful experience of worship. Leaving the mountaintop and on the way down into the valley, they encountered an epileptic boy in need of help. They saw a need and responded. That's community. Leaving the place of worship and encountering human suffering and need is the reality of the church. Responding like Jesus is the challenge to the church.

The story of the Good Samaritan[11] is about a victim of crime. Jesus taught us that unfortunately those in the church are often too busy or too unconcerned to reach out to those in need. In this story, two religious people pass by a man victimized by crime, while leaving the man's rescue to a Samaritan, one who did not have ties to the temple. Community ministry is for people of faith to reach out to the needs of others as they travel the Jericho roads of their daily lives.

As a young boy, Jesus was in the temple learning at the feet of teachers.[12] However, He did not stay there. The account indicates that He went back home where He grew in favor with God and others.[13] If we want to understand the ministry of Jesus, we must pay attention to how He spent His time, both in the temple and in the community. Far more is written about what He did outside the temple than what He did in the temple. An inventory of what the modern church says about itself probably would contain more information about what goes on inside its walls than on the outside. If that is true, the extent to which it is true is an indictment of the modern church. New Testament ministry was community ministry. Community ministry occurs when and where the church encounters the needs of a broken humanity and addresses them with compassionate care.

Examples of Community Ministry

The assumption should not be made that the church is not making an impact outside its walls. There are numerous examples, probably in every community, of churches involved in extending a hand of compassion, yet the possibilities for creating new approaches are unlimited.

The Baptist Hospital in Montgomery, Alabama, through its foundation, has set up a healthcare clinic for the working poor who have no healthcare coverage. This clinic—now separated from the Baptist Hospital—is staffed by people from churches who give their time, resources, and expertise to provide a healthcare ministry to the working poor without regard to their faith. This ministry is an example of a coalition of churches, having a similar vision and with the initial help of the Baptist Hospital Foundation, reaching out to the health needs of the working poor—to families, to children, mothers, and fathers. This specialized ministry, in one perspective, is not very different from the ministry of healing that Jesus demonstrated when He was here walking among people and doing good.[14]

The three Baptist institutions of higher learning in Alabama are all modeling outreach outside their campuses. David Potts, president of Judson College, an all-female college in one of the poorest communities in the nation, stated that this college is affected by what goes on outside its campus and thus must tear down the walls and reach out to the needs of the community. As a result, Potts has served in numerous ways, including chairperson of the committee for selecting the police chief of Marion, Alabama. Even more significantly, he has been a leader in Sowing Seeds of Hope, Inc., which is a coalition of government, community, and church leaders coming together to address the economic needs of this impoverished county, including the search for jobs, job training, childcare, decent and affordable housing, and other activities that would contribute toward economic development.

Tom Corts, president of Samford University in Birmingham, Alabama, has been on the forefront in leading the state of Alabama to move from an antiquated state constitution that hurts the poor and rewards the rich to a new state constitution. He serves as chairperson of a coalition of concerned citizens who wish to change the way the state of Alabama does business through its current constitution. Their desire is to bring equity and fairness to the fundamental body of law for the state so that citizens are treated justly and fairly.

The University of Mobile in Prichard, Alabama, also has been reaching out to the city. Mark Foley, president of the University of Mobile, has worked with the city of Prichard to provide strategic planning and leadership. He serves on a key advisory board that seeks to bring new economic life to the beleaguered community. Foley and his fellow Baptist educators are examples of three leaders of Christian institutions of higher learning seeking to make their communities more of what Christ would have them to be. They are using both traditional and non-traditional approaches in an effort to minister to the communities in which God has placed them.

At Eden Westside Baptist Church in Pell City, Alabama, the pastor and congregation have a vision that every member is a minister. They have a significant outreach ministry as well as a ministry to people in the church, intentionally building a good, balanced model that can be made available to other churches. Their vision involves a community of care where broken people can find healing, forgiveness, and redemption. On this fifty-eight-acre campus, they envision a drug treatment facility, housing for people with drug addictions, a center that will help to prevent teenage pregnancy, a referral center for community resources that are currently available, and housing for the elderly. There is a sense of excitement and commitment to a concept of ministry that embraces the entire community.

Interfaith Hospitality Network is a national organization that sets up standards for churches in working with the homeless. A coalition of churches in Birmingham, Alabama, working under these national standards, has responded to homeless families by providing shelter inside their own church buildings on a rotating basis. Each church houses homeless families for twelve weeks at a time, providing food, shelter, childcare, job search, and any other particular needs of the individual families. The advantage to this approach is that homeless people are served in buildings that normally are used for less than five hours a week, so no new construction is required. This arrangement also provides church members with an on-campus way to minister to families who really need help. It also provides ways for churches of different faiths to come together with a common mission.

The Government Street Presbyterian Church in Mobile, Alabama, has been providing breakfast for homeless people five days a week for the past twelve years. The members of the congregation rotate through various responsibilities in preparing a hot breakfast for as many as seventy-five people daily. This church has been well known throughout the community for its outreach to the homeless.

The Good Samaritan Program, a crime victims program in Mobile, Alabama, was developed in partnership with the District Attorney's office, the Mobile Police Department, and Volunteers of America, Southeast. Volunteers of America developed a relationship with a number of churches, soliciting volunteers to become "Good Samaritans." The Good Samaritans are trained to respond to the unique needs of people who have been traumatized by crime. The Mobile Police Department notifies Volunteers of America staff day and night about victims of crime, and the Good Samaritans are commissioned to respond directly by offering prayer, providing emotional support, repairing a broken window or door, or meeting whatever needs they encounter.

Possibilities are limited only by one's vision, creativity, and commitment. Each year, what if every five-hundred-member church decided to help one family of low income to become homeowners? Smaller churches could form working coalitions of four or five churches to do likewise. The crises in housing for low-income individuals would be greatly affected.

What if each church adopted a homeless family? What if it provided the family a place to stay and helped them transition to a more permanent house while assisting in providing meaningful employment and training as well as childcare and transportation? Many churches have the capacity for this kind of community ministry.

What if every church adopted a welfare mom, provided mentoring, job training, and employment? The Bible studies and spiritual training could be a natural part of the ministry. What if every church decided that it would minister to children whose parents were not available? Love and nurturing are natural needs of children, which could be provided by substitute parents. Such love would have a lifetime impact on children with such needs.

Harold L. Rutledge—An Example

Harold L. Rutledge was a long-term professor at New Orleans Baptist Theological Seminary. He was a Christian man who lived out his faith not only in the church and on the campus but also in relationships. He knew about redemption and the possibilities of people. On that foundation he majored, and a difference was made. He provided on-campus counseling in addition to counseling unwed mothers at Seller's Home for Unwed Mothers. Wherever he went, he created a caring, nurturing environment.

Not only did Rutledge provide an example of ministry, he also taught the importance of interpersonal relations and sought to describe what it took to have meaningful interpersonal relationships. He developed what he termed "25 Structural Factors of Relationships." Through these words, he sought to describe what constitutes an interpersonal relationship.

Structural Factors of Relationships

- Warmth of emotional regard—love—affection
- Demonstrativeness—companionship
- Interpersonal interdependence
- Trust (not a prediction of behavior)
- Interest—concern—awareness. Hearing more than is said.
- Communication—verbal and non-verbal
- Affirmation
- Focused optimism—expectations
- Unconditional acceptance
- Respect—esteem
- Openness—genuineness, sincerity (not deceitful)
- Realism—tolerance

- Patience—peace
- Humility—Allowing the other person to be right, to have a will, to be an equal.
- Courage
- Persistence (not to be confused with nagging). Not characteristically a quitter.
- Honesty
- Knowledge (of each other)
- Aspiration for maturity
- Commitment
- "At-easeness"—comfortable, relaxed, and tranquil in the presence of the other person (not needing to defend or attack)
- Consistency—regularity—predictability
- Stimulation
- Sacrifice—self-giving—suffering
- Intimacy (not synonymous with sex). Closest possible togetherness.

For Rutledge, each of these concepts described an essential part of interpersonal relationships and described how Jesus Himself related to the community and to individuals. Rutledge taught that all of life is about interpersonal relationships, and interpersonal relationships will be the determining factor as to how successful one will be in life.[15]

Interpersonal Relationships—The Key to Ministry

Our ability to form meaningful, caring relationships and our commitment to those relationships will determine our effectiveness in ministry inside and outside the walls of the church. To a broken community, the need for a meaningful relationship probably is greater than that of a thirsty man for a drink of water, and what better place for that interpersonal relationship to come from than the church—the body of Christ. As you go into the community, be a friend, just as Christ has been a friend.

CHAPTER 20

How to Work with Other Helping Professionals

Loretta G. Rivers

A pastor in a rural area called my office one afternoon in a desperate search for help for a young teenager in his church. The teenager was in a crisis situation and had turned first to the pastor for help. The teenager's parents were on the way to the church, and the pastor wanted to have some suggestions for them. The pastor was unfamiliar with the resources and helping professionals in his area and did not know where to seek help. If the pastor had established working relationships with other helping professionals in the community, he likely would have been able to locate assistance more quickly.

The purpose of this chapter is to provide ministers with basic information about working with other helping professionals. This information is useful for several reasons. First, establishing relationships with helping professionals provides opportunities for ministry. Second, knowledgeable ministers are able to network with other helping professionals. Third, guidelines for working together help ministers maintain positive relationships with other professionals. Finally, interested ministers and helping professionals are provided various opportunities to work together.

Opportunities for Ministry

Establishing relationships with helping professionals in the community provides opportunities for ministry. Because the church is a part of the local community, the people in the church should show that they care about the community. Ministers who take the time to get to know helping professionals provide positive examples of caring about the needs of people. Ministers and church members who demonstrate concern for others show evidence of Christ's love.

Building relationships with other professionals can benefit those whom the minister serves. When a person seeks help, the minister has resources available to utilize when the problem is beyond his or her knowledge or expertise. Thus, ministers can guide persons to resources more quickly and efficiently. In addition, the helping professional identifies ministers and congregations as potential parts of a person's support system.

Working with helping professionals also can provide opportunities for ministry outside of the church. As professionals identify the needs of clients, the minister can evaluate the church's ability to respond to those needs. As the church develops ministries, the church enlarges its contact with people and increases its impact on individual lives.

Networking

Networking involves making contact with persons and building relationships so that information, resources, and expertise may be shared.[1] Networking, optimally, benefits all persons involved. Such activities as building a resource file, conducting a community needs assessment, and offering the church as a meeting place provide opportunities for ministers to get to know other helping professionals.

An adult education minister noticed several of the adults in her church were facing difficult decisions involving their aging parents. In an effort to find educational materials that might inform and encourage the adult children, she contacted professionals at local agencies serving the elderly. The minister discovered that these professionals were available and willing to speak to members of her church. Her networking efforts led to the implementation of an educational series titled "Decision

Making and Aging Parents." The church provided a safe and supportive place for persons to share their fears and concerns with one another.

As ministers network, they should create a resource file of service providers. A resource file contains information about helping professionals, social service agencies, churches, printed materials, and other resources available to meet specific needs. Some community agencies publish resource directories or make them available via the Internet. Ministers can develop resource files specific to their areas of ministry by contacting local social service agencies, city and county government offices, and churches and denominational agencies that provide services to the target group. Internet search engines, the yellow pages, and library databases contain additional information. When adding professional or community agencies to the resource file, ministers should make personal contacts whenever possible. Such associations will be valuable if assistance is needed at a later time. Ministers also should request and review any printed materials about each professional or agency. Each listing in the resource file should include the name of the professional or agency, the address, the telephone number, and the services provided. In order to maintain a useful and accurate file, periodic contact with professionals in the resource file is essential.

A community needs assessment is an additional way to network with other helping professionals. A community needs assessment is an extensive examination and evaluation of community needs and available resources with the purpose of prioritizing problems and identifying possible solutions. Churches can use community needs assessments to determine opportunities for ministry. Helping professionals can provide some of the most valuable information about a community.

The assessment requires planning and preparation. When interviewing helping professionals, interviewers should explain the purpose of the study and make appointments in advance. Interviews should last no longer than thirty minutes. Interviewers should prepare questions in advance and, if possible, send a copy to interviewees prior to the interview date. Sample questions include: What is your agency's purpose? What services do you provide? What needs do your clients have? What are additional needs that are not being met? How can churches in the community assist you or your agency?

Several students and I participated in an association-wide community needs assessment in the Greater New Orleans area. Volunteers interviewed a variety of community leaders, including city officials, social workers, and agency directors. Reactions to the survey were overwhelmingly positive. Many leaders expressed appreciation that church members cared enough to ask about community needs. My team interviewed the director of social services at a large hospital. When asked what churches could do to meet the needs of her clients, she replied, "Provide a meeting place for cancer support groups." This opportunity for ministry probably would not have been identified without contact with the helping professional.

An additional way to network with helping professionals is by attending or hosting continuing education programs. Most helping professionals have to attend continuing education programs yearly to maintain their professional certification or license. Ministers also can attend programs that may be of interest to them. In addition to knowledge, the programs provide an opportunity to network with other professionals who have similar interests.

Churches also can host continuing education programs. Churches are ideal places to discuss spiritual and religious issues. Spirituality and religion have been increasingly topics of interest in the helping fields. In addition, the community has an opportunity to learn about the church when attending educational programs at the church.

Guidelines for Working Together

Ministers and helping professionals should follow some basic guidelines to develop and maintain positive working relationships. The development of healthy patterns of communication is necessary for a good working relationship. Open and honest communication is essential. Honest evaluation and feedback contribute to a healthy working relationship. Both professionals need the freedom to express their thoughts without fearing criticism.

In addition, ministers and helping professionals need to maintain periodic contact to stay aware of any changes and to sustain the relationship. The frequency of contact will depend upon the level of collaboration between the minister and the professional. A phone call, an e-mail, or a short note two or three times a year is usually sufficient interaction. These contacts promote ongoing communication.

Ministers and helping professionals need to seek common areas of agreement. Ministers and professionals will disagree at times. To work together, both groups may need to set aside differences that may hinder working relationships. Individuals should seek opportunities to work together that do not compromise the basic goals of either person. Both professionals should be concerned about the best interests of the person they are serving and should be willing to work together whenever possible.

Ministers also should respect the expertise, knowledge, and skills of other professionals. Helping professionals have specialized training and are equipped to meet the needs of persons in various life circumstances. Ministers should learn about the roles of different professionals and recognize the contributions of each in the helping process.

Finally, ministers should consider working with other helping professionals who may not hold the same beliefs. These professionals may have clients who are members of the minister's church or denomination. Ministers may have opportunities to provide information to helping professionals that help facilitate work with the client. The minister and his/her church may serve as a support system that enables a client to get through a time of crisis. Without having contact with the minister, the helping professional may not have recognized the important role of the church as a supportive network.

Opportunities for Ministers and Helping Professionals to Work Together

Ministers and helping professionals can work together in varying degrees of cooperation. Ministers may have little contact with the helping professional if contact is initiated on a referral basis only. On a consultation basis, ministers and helping professionals work more closely together as they exchange information to help the client. The greatest degree of contact between ministers and helping professionals takes place on a collaboration basis when both are working together with the client or on behalf of the client as co-participants in the helping process.

Ministers may refer clients to helping professionals or vice versa. Referrals allow clients to utilize other service providers. When making a referral, the minister should discuss with the client potential resources for service, give information about each provider, and assist the client in making a choice among services.[2]

The minister should not make the decision for the client but should provide information and guidance that helps the client make his or her own decision. Once a client chooses a resource, the minister or client may make contact with the service provider. Most referral sources require some basic information when initiating contact. Information required may include the name, address, and phone number of the person seeking services; the reason for the referral; a brief description of the problem; and the name of the person making the referral. If the minister makes the referral, he or she should inquire whether the client meets service criteria and what the client needs to do to receive services. If the client makes his or her own referral, the minister should give the person contact information for the service provider and follow up with the client to see if he or she makes contact.

Ministers also may receive referrals from other helping professionals. When receiving referrals, ministers or designated office staff should obtain, at minimum, the name and contact information for the client, the reason for referral, and the name and contact information for the referral source. Timely follow-up on referrals is necessary. Ministers and churches will develop positive reputations among helping professionals when referrals are handled appropriately and efficiently.

Consultation is another way that ministers and helping professionals may work together. Consultation involves the utilization of another professional's knowledge, expertise, or skills. Consultants can provide additional information in specialized areas.[3] The consultation process is usually short-term. The minister should evaluate the need for consultation, choose among available consultants, and help the client effectively utilize the consultant's services.[4]

The minister also can be a consultant. Helping professionals may not have the expertise or training to deal with particular spiritual issues that may be important to the client. The helping professional may contact a minister for suggestions on how best to assist the client with problems on issues related to spiritual matters.

An additional way ministers and helping professionals can work together is on a collaboration basis. Collaboration refers to a process wherein the minister and helping professional work together as partners in the helping process.[5] Collaboration is more time intensive than consultation or referrals. Ministers and helping professionals may work together on a team that evaluates and serves the client. For example, a hospital chaplain may meet weekly with other health professionals on a rehabilitation unit to discuss the progress of patients and develop care plans that address the holistic needs of patients. Ministers may serve on institutional ethics committees that address ethical issues related to clients. Ministers and counselors or social workers may work together as co-therapists. One example wherein clergy and clinicians have worked as co-therapists is with survivors of childhood traumatic abuse who value their religious beliefs as an important resource.[6]

Ministers can choose the degree to which they want to work with other helping professionals. Contact and cooperation with other professionals can provide opportunities for ministry and can be beneficial to ministers and churches even on a limited basis. Ministers need to network with professionals in the community to establish positive relationships. Ministers can maintain relationships with helping professionals through open and honest communication, respect for other professionals, and periodic contact.

CHAPTER 21

Decision Making

Jeanine Cannon Bozeman

One of the greatest gifts God has given us is the ability to weigh our options and make a choice. A large part of our life is determined by our ability to make up our mind. Living well demands that we make good decisions. According to John Homer Miller, "Men fail, not because they are stupid, but because they are not decisively impassioned."[1] The poet James Russell Lowell expresses the importance of decisions: "Our lives are the sum total of our decisions and their consequences. Character is the finished product of our choices, crystallized, set, hardened into a pattern."[2]

The Bible and Decision Making

The Bible contains the stories of many persons who made decisions, some good and some bad. Eve made a decision to eat of the forbidden fruit.[3] Abraham chose to leave his home and become a pilgrim.[4] Reflecting on Abraham's decision, Vance Havner challenges each of us to become pilgrims, interested in our heavenly destination.[5]

Lot decided to settle in Sodom. He is a good example of a good person who made a bad choice.[6] In contrast, Moses decided to renounce the pleasures of Egypt and choose to suffer affliction with the people of God. He could have decided to enjoy a life of luxury and ease, but he chose to be faithful to God.[7]

Joshua made up his mind to serve the Lord regardless of the

choice others made. He was courageous in his declaration.[8] David's decision to commit adultery with Bathsheba and to arrange the murder of her husband, Uriah, was abominable.[9] Esther decided to respond to the challenge Mordecai present- ed to her, and she spoke up for her people instead of playing it safe. She risked her life to appeal to King Ahasuerus on behalf of the Jewish people.[10] On the other hand, Peter made a decision to deny Christ.[11]

Ruth chose to follow Naomi instead of returning to her native people. She pledged her loyalty to her mother-in-law and her God.[12] Yet Judas chose to betray Christ for thirty pieces of silver.[13] Jesus chose the way of sacrifice for us, giving his life on Calvary that we may have eternal life.[14]

Life Experience of Decision Making

Along with examples from the Bible, we learn many lessons about decisions from our own life experiences. They teach us that decisions are necessary and often difficult, and that they have consequences. In working at a home for unwed mothers while a seminary student, I saw many young, pregnant girls who learned that the choices they made had consequences, some of them far-reaching and painful.

Fear causes some persons to have a tough time making deci- sions. They may be afraid they will make a mistake and suffer the consequences of a wrong choice. Having two or more choices may paralyze them. Losing the approval of others may frighten them away from choosing. They may have the irra- tional belief that they must be loved and approved of by every- one for everything all the time. Still others are slow to make decisions because they are afraid that their decisions may have a negative impact on members of their family or their friends.

Other variables can stand in the way. Often persons are blocked in their decision making by irrational beliefs, second guessing, anticipation of something better, and option blind- ness. Additional blockers may include a problem with depres- sion, a lack of priorities, an absence of self-confidence, or low self-esteem. Being unwilling to sacrifice anything or wanting it all also can block people from making a decision. Occasionally persons lose touch with their feelings, which also can contribute to indecision.

In order to identify your personal decision blockers, you may find it helpful to examine the messages you have received from parents and/or authority figures regarding major issues such as money, sex, education, work ethic, or other life issues. Although we are not victims of our upbringing, our past may heavily influence the decisions we make unless we consciously choose to free ourselves from early messages that may no longer be appropriate or useful.

According to Theodore I. Rubin, people often make pseudodecisions to avoid making real decisions. Pseudodecisions may come in the form of procrastination, ambivalence, impulse moves, or inappropriate dependency. They also can be reflected in going against the tide, trying to work all the options, looking back, foot dragging, and wondering what might have been.[15] By contrast, a real decision is "a free, unconditional, total and personal commitment to a choice or option, or a group of them."[16] Real decision making is marked by strong feelings and is based on investments of time, energy, talent, and resources. In other words, the choice is a full commitment to a favored option.[17]

Three Major Decisions

Each of us faces many decisions that influence the success and happiness of our life, but three major decisions are crucial for an effective and fulfilling life. The first decision is who or what will be the master of our life. This decision not only determines our level of living, it also determines our destiny for eternity. Some persons choose pleasure and find their lives seeking new thrills. Others choose status or prestige and give themselves to pursuing achievements as a goal. Still others choose material possessions and so attempt to accumulate wealth. Our best choice, however, is to follow Christ.[18]

The second major decision has to do with marriage, Will I marry and, if so, who will be my mate? I have noticed that some people choose to marry the wrong person, someone who is totally incompatible and headed in an opposite direction. They have no unity in their goals in life. Other people choose to marry the right person at the wrong time, perhaps when the timing is inappropriate for such a major decision to be successful.

A third major decision concerns mission or purpose in life. As a therapist I have seen many miserable persons who felt that their lives were meaningless. Laurie Beth Jones stresses the value of a personal mission statement. She insists that it can have a direct impact on how we work. "Once you are clear about what you were put here to do, then jobs become only a means toward your mission, not an end in themselves."[19]

Improving as Decision Makers

Persons may have emotional collapses because they cannot make decisions. The reassuring fact, however, is that decision making can be learned. It can be cultivated with practice and improved.

Most of us can benefit from improving our decision-making skills by developing a strategy that goes a long way toward demystifying the process. Rubin describes a strategy for arriving at a good decision that could prove helpful to us. The strategy involves brainstorming the possibilities, reflecting on each of them emotionally as well as intellectually, processing them in light of life concerns, settling on one choice out of all of the possibilities, and taking action that shows a commitment to the choice.[20]

Granted, while this approach is helpful, the success of it depends on a person's being able to articulate his or her life concerns. He or she must also be a person who has a healthy self-concept.[21]

T. B. Maston insists that making good decisions begins with a mature way of thinking about life itself.[22] Some people think about life in a way that is somewhat impulsive. Others are guided by social mores and traditions. Still others live according to a moral code. The way of thinking about life for a Christian, however, is influenced by a sense of God's guidance and biblical principles.[23]

At the heart of decision making is the ability to determine whether a choice is right or wrong. According to Maston, we can make such a critical determination if we consider the outcome of our choice on us personally. We also have to consider the consequences of our decision on other people. Moreover, we have to consider the impact of our choice on our mission as Christians in the world.[24]

Another way to determine whether a decision is right or wrong is to ask ourselves if we would be embarrassed if anyone found out about the choice we made. We could also ask ourselves if other people would make the same choice and feel good about it. Most important, we could ask ourselves if we would feel comfortable sharing our choice with God in prayer.[25]

In the process of making a good decision, God gives us His guidance. As Maston indicates, one of the ways He guides us is by giving us impressions about the choice we should make. Another way is by showing us biblical principles that relate to our decision. Yet another way is by responding to us when we talk with Him in prayer about our choice.[26]

We know that one of the most difficult parts of living and maturing is making right, moral decisions. Isaiah 30:21 gives us assurance that God will be with us as we make choices. The challenge for us is to think carefully and make wise personal decisions.

Decisions are necessary, they are difficult, and they have consequences. Each of us will eventually sit down to a banquet of consequences. May our banquet be one of happiness, not sorrow; peace, not regret; joy, not despair. May all of us dine as children of the King!

CHAPTER 22

A Church Touching the Community: A Testimony

W. Dan Parker

Introduction

I had been a pastor on the field in rural North Carolina only a few months when Anna called. I had met her a few weeks earlier in the joint Vacation Bible School in our small farm community. She was calling to invite me to give the invocation at the opening day of the 1961 tobacco auction at her husband's warehouse nearby. Without hesitation I accepted the invitation, thinking that a pastor ought to be involved with the community in which he served. Even though the United States Surgeon General had just a few weeks earlier made his first ruling on the hazards of cigarette smoking, I led the prayer. I had wondered whether I should pray that this tobacco would cause no one cancer or just thank God for the harvest. I do not know of any particular results of this "community service," but it launched a ministry in which I have continually been involved in the communities wherever I have served.

Touching a Small Town on the Edge of Suburbia

Later, I was pastor of a small town on the outer edges of a metropolitan city. Like other such towns, it provided many opportunities for community involvement. It was my people's town, so they were already involved as citizens. My first venture in community relationships there was during the height of the Vietnam War and corresponding protest movements. Our high school students wanted to present a more positive patriotic image of youth in the late sixties, so they came to me with the idea of holding an all-day youth patriotic rally in the heart of town. They called it "Operation: Up, Up With America." I became their leader and cheerleader for the summer of 1968. They gained the involvement of teens from other churches and races, which, for the times, was a major feat. Politicians, musicians, bands, and radio-TV personalities were invited and participated, encouraging these enthusiastic and patriotic youth. This event gave me a taste for such involvement in the community again.

A Church in a Community in Transition in a Large City

In my next pastorate, I served a city church in an old community that was going through major economic and racial transition. The part of the city in which the church was located was also facing major changes in the commercial and shopping areas. Adult bookstores, strip bars, and street-walking prostitution were taking over nearby. Our people were doing all they knew how to do to resist such an invasion in their quiet residential community. They asked me to accompany them to a court hearing at city hall where the city solicitor was fighting bathhouses, which were known fronts for prostitution. I drove the bus and became the leader of this small moral army that included several people from other churches. At city hall we were dismayed by events in the courtroom, so we decided to go see the mayor. As we expected, the mayor could not see us, but we did hope to register our concern for the community. One of his aides came out and met with us and assured us that our concerns were being heard. He was a nice Christian man who spoke as though he shared our feelings about the issue.

The next week this aide to the mayor called and asked me to serve on the Mayor's Religious Advisory Committee, on which I served until I left that city. I met the president of the Christian Council of the city while serving on this advisory committee and became involved in this community interfaith group. During this time I became concerned about the need for a chaplain's program at the city's airport, which was a major aviation hub and international airport. I became aware of one man's struggle to have a chapel at the airport. An airplane had been hijacked the day before our monthly meeting with the mayor. This incident made obvious the need for a full-time chaplain at the airport in addition to a chapel. I brought my concern to the mayor and was subsequently appointed as his liaison in developing such a ministry and facility. My first task was to meet with the Top Committee of Airlines that operated the airport. A new terminal was under construction, and my task was to request of this committee that they allot space for an interfaith prayer chapel in the new facility. The Christian Council would be responsible for establishing and overseeing the chaplain's program. At the meeting with the Top Committee, I was told by the director that all of the space in the terminal had already been spoken for and that there was no room for such a chapel. He offered the obligatory words of agreement that such a facility and program were needed, but he also offered the strong insistence that it was not possible.

At the next meeting with the mayor I brought a report on what the Top Committee had said. The mayor confidently said in the meeting, "There is no way that the largest airport in the world does not have space for a small prayer chapel. I assure you, Rev. Parker, that as mayor of this city I have something to say about that. I promise you there will be a prayer chapel." That was in 1978, and until this day there is both a chapel and a chaplain on duty twenty-four hours a day. This experience gave me the opportunity to see unfolding the results of the involvement of Christian people in their community and with their city government in a way none of us could have imagined. The struggle against the immoral plight was only partially and temporarily successful, but the church had been involved and continued working diligently with others in the community.

A Suburban Church Touching Its Community

My next pastoral service was in a community with a very

complex identity. There were many churches and a number of schools. Our church was at the intersection of the mail routes of three cities. It was difficult to do much more than just try to be in the community through the schools and sports programs. Because of my children and their involvement in the schools and sports, I found a way to influence the community. First, I became involved with the Little League team on which my son played. I was first an assistant coach and then coach of his team for several years. Others in the church became involved, and we also reached people in the programs who became Christians and church members.

When my son became a member of the high school football team, his coach asked me to serve as chaplain, a role many pastors and youth ministers often fill in their communities and children's schools. Such involvement became the doorway to a positive image for the church in the area. Our church had fed the football team of the nearby high school and now was doing it again, as we served the pre-game meal.

During the twelve years I served this congregation, our church hosted a fall festival at Halloween, giving families in the community a safe alternative to trick-or-treating, which even in the early 1980s had become a dangerous adventure for children. Our people refused to take pay for anything at the festival. Merchants contributed various items, and the people paid the expenses. This generosity made our people known and appreciated in the suburban community and also gave them a strong feeling of worth among their own neighbors. The church had not had many opportunities to touch its community beyond traditional visitation and a preschool program, but the fall festival sent a very positive message to the neighborhood.

A Small Town Church in Suburbia

All of these experiences of relating to the community served to prepare me for the most fruitful and exciting of all my adventures in taking the church into the community. The church I now have served for more than ten years has moved to a new level of community involvement. I serve as pastor of a church in a small suburban town where urban decay is catching up to us and suburban sprawl has moved at least twenty-five miles beyond us. Mostly because of racial transition, the church had been in decline for nearly ten years when I became pastor. The town has become primarily a tourist village, being near a large and popular tourist attraction that is one of the leading parks in the country. The town is more than 150 years old, and the local shops and stores have been replaced by gift shops, craft stores, and other businesses usually found in an area frequently visited by tourists.

When I met with the search committee, I asked them what opinion the people of the town had of the church. The chairman said that our new associational missionary, in consulting with them, had visited in shops and asked that same question. "Many," he said, "gave negative answers." The overriding sentiment of those interviewed was that First Baptist is "a church that buys property and fires preachers." Our church had bought two large parcels of land in the town at two different times as a future location of the church. They had fired the previous pastor and a staff member about a year before I came to serve there. The community had good reason for such a description of our church.

Upon beginning ministry there, I knew it was necessary to get out and meet the merchants in the nearby stores and begin trying to change the image of the church. As I did so, I was disappointed to learn that most of these people lived outside of our community. They were attached to the town, but only though their business interests. Still, it was a helpful beginning that has paid off richly over the years.

Not long after I began as pastor of the church, the leaders of the merchants came to me and asked if our church would host their annual arts and crafts festival, held every Father's Day weekend on our three-acre field in the heart of town. When I presented this request to our leaders, I experienced some hesitation and negative reactions from some prominent people. They acquiesced, however, when they realized that most of our leaders saw value in such a venture with the town merchants and believed it was a good opportunity to improve their relationship with the community.

This was the beginning of a new day for First Baptist Church and its town. I had learned that the former city manager had been hard on the church in the past, and some of our people still had negative feeling toward the city. The merchants would be the buffer. About the same time, the mayor and her husband, both church members elsewhere, began attending our church. This situation soon began to create a whole new attitude between our church and city hall. The mayor had not been in office when all of the negative things happened, so she brought the promise of a new relationship with the city government.

Often, during revival meetings, we invited the merchants to a special night for recognition and appreciation. We did the same for the city employees and police. In fact, there have been several occasions when we invited and recognized leaders and politicians from the town and county governments. One such occasion was the kick-off for our 1996 Olympics ministry. Since three of the events were to be held in a nearby park, our denomination asked our church to host an Olympic hospitality center on our three-acre vacant field, called by some "the Village Green."

Kick-off Sunday was an exciting day. With the various dignitaries and guests, our people were beginning to envision what could be. This was the birth of an exciting ministry with many opportunities for involvement with the people of our town. Already we had been hosting a fall festival at Halloween on that vacant field, just as we had done in my previous church. The city was very helpful in providing services that enabled us to do a better job with the festival, especially with police and security.

We were now coming to be known as "the church that does the fall festival." Besides this festival, we host an outdoor concert on July 4 on our field, which is an ideal viewing place for the Fourth of July fireworks from the park, adjacent to the town. This event began when a merchant asked us to host a large community-wide yard sale to raise funds for a young quadriplegic man who had grown up in the town. After the sale, many of us gathered on the sight and watched the July 4 fireworks from the nearby park. The idea was born there to host a concert each year that would be concluded by the fireworks. Another event is a community-wide Easter egg hunt for children. Our people put out thousands of eggs each year, plus give a prize to every child attending. We use it as a time to share the Gospel through stories and also to keep a file of names and addresses.

We never charge people to come to these events. Many people see the Christian church as an organization that is always asking for money. Our intention is to be a giving church, not a receiving church. The spirit we seek to convey at every event is that we are a loving, ministering, and giving people. We give because Christ gave to us. We love others because He loves us.

The Olympic ministry was one that lit the fire of ministry enthusiasm in our people. We built a large pavilion to house the Olympic hospitality center and, it was planned, to serve our church in the future as a recreation facility. Churches and youth groups from thirty-five or forty churches came to our town and ministry site during the five weeks of the Olympics and Paralympics. We were involved with our state convention, the International and North American Mission Boards, as well as our association and neighboring churches during these events. Many of our people were volunteers and had trained well for the ministry they would be doing. We expected to host people from all over the world.

The Olympic torch was to come to our town for its last stop before the opening ceremony. The town leaders asked us to provide the entertainment for the crowd, which was expected on Main Street near our pavilion around 11:00 P.M., with the torch-bearer due about 12:30 P.M. Police estimated the crowd by midnight at thirty thousand. Our group, from churches across the Southeast and two colleges, ministered more than they could ever have imagined. The torch did not arrive until 4:00 A.M., enabling these students to entertain the people for five hours. The leaders in the town were amazed that we were able to provide so much top quality entertainment for such a long time.

After the Olympics and Paralympics were over, our people

longed for an opportunity to continue such a ministry. They had invested more than $65,000 in building the pavilion and believed that the type of ministry we had provided for nearly six weeks should not stop. They began praying and petitioning our state convention leaders and area associational missionaries to allow us to continue a meaningful ministry in our resort town. We were met with open arms by each agency. This ministry would continue. We knew we could not handle such a task alone, furnishing the needed finances and manpower. We consequently formed a partnership with our state convention, the North American Mission Board, and several associations and churches in our area. God put us in touch with a full-time home missionary needing an assignment, and we were on the way. The ministry is now in its fifth year. It provides volunteers for city projects, special events like a gift-wrap ministry during Christmas for shoppers in our village, carolers from churches that partner with us, and special work crews when needed by either the city or merchants' association. This ministry provides volunteers for many attractions and events at the nearby park and recently began a ministry in the campground during the camping season. Also, a part-time chaplain from the ministry serves employees and patrons in the park.

Several years ago, during the crises in Bosnia and Kosovo, many refugees began pouring into our town. Because of our church's reputation for ministry and giving, the agency responsible for these refugees called on us to provide English classes and other ministries to these people. An after-school program for refugee children was begun in which tutoring and help with language is given to the elementary and middle school children. Our church, which had been declining for more than fifteen years, is now growing again, with numerous nationalities becoming a part of the fellowship. Our children's and youth ministries are growing again.

In 2001, nearly two hundred men and women converged on our town for a W.M.U. Missions Fest, sponsored by the state convention, our ministry, and our resort missionary. These people performed many ministries in the apartment complexes and for the merchants, and they met many needs that weekend in our town. This effort was another testimony to the church's impact on its community.

In all of these experiences, especially the last one, it has been obvious that God has been at work. His timing has been evident throughout. Our church has come to be known as a servant church, focusing on giving, and never asking from the people of our town. We are no longer known as "the church that buys property and fires preachers." The church gave eleven acres of that land it had bought, with $550,000 invested, to a black congregation that had been meeting there for several years. What a joy it is when the church learns that "it is more blessed to give than to receive"[1] and takes seriously the second Great Commandment, "Thou shalt love thy neighbor as thyself."[2]

Conclusion:
Strengthening Your
Interpersonal Relationship Skills

Healthy relationships provide a secure setting for effective ministry. For that reason, a minister does well to give serious attention to developing the skills necessary for strengthening interpersonal relationships. In the previous chapters, some of the basic skills have been described, along with some very good ideas about how you can strengthen them so you can be more effective in the ministry setting to which God calls you.

Reading about interpersonal relationship skills, however, can help you only if you intend to put what you have read into practice. If you don't, you will be like the person who tries to learn how to change a flat tire only by reading a book on the subject. While it's a good start, it cannot substitute for actually opening the trunk of the car, finding the necessary tools, and working with them to change the tire.

Similarly, reading about the ways a minister can nurture healthy relationships is definitely a good start. But it cannot replace the necessary work of putting what you have read into practice so you can strengthen your interpersonal relationship skills.

To help you put the insights you have encountered in this book into practice, consider the following steps. They may be simple to understand, but they may be a little more difficult to take. But give it a try. Take one step at a time, and don't give up along the way.

The first step is to take inventory of your relationships.

Specifically, ask God to show you the relationships in your life that need to be strengthened.

As the arrangement of the articles in this book has indicated, an inventory of your relationships starts from the inside out, beginning with your relationship with the Lord. Is your relationship with Him changing, deepening, maturing, and growing more intimate? How does it need to be strengthened?

What about your relationship with yourself? Ask the Lord to show you the ways in which you need to grow toward maturity in terms of your self-concept and the extent to which you have appropriated His blessing in Christ into your life and ministry.

Are the relationships with your family helping you or hurting you? Seek the Lord's direction as you take personal inventory of the blessings as well as the struggles associated with the family of your childhood and adolescent years.

How strong are your relationships with the people in your home? Give the Lord a chance to open your eyes to the ways He wants you to strengthen your marriage. Let Him show you what you can do to be a better parent. Moreover, allow Him to reveal to you the ways your family relationships can be strengthened in your present ministry setting.

Is God pleased with the relationships you are nurturing with the people in your congregation? The Lord can help you to take stock of the relationships you are nurturing with church leaders, staff members, and others in the congregation. He can enable you to isolate the areas of improvement.

What community relationships do you need to work on in order to be an effective minister to the people outside the walls of your church? The Lord calls us to a ministry setting so we will extend His love to the people there. He can show us the relationships in our communities that need attention.

The second step is to evaluate how well you have developed some of the basic interpersonal relationship skills. In the articles, some of the basic skills have been addressed. Use the following list in your evaluation of the interpersonal relationship skills you are incorporating into your ministry now. Determine how well you think you have developed them.

- Communicating
- Listening
- Asserting yourself
- Forgiving
- Dealing with difficult people
- Managing conflict
- Relating to people in the community
- Making wise decisions

Of course, this list of skills is not exhaustive. It suggests some of the basic skills ministers will want to develop as we work with others to accomplish Kingdom tasks together.

The third step is to take action. This is probably the most difficult step of all; you can't skip it if you intend to grow as a minister. If God has shown you some relationships that need to be strengthened, your best choice is to respond to His direction and address them. If you have isolated a relationship skill that you need to develop more, take the initiative and put the skill to work in your relationships.

The fourth step is to entrust your relationships and the skills needed to strengthen them to the Lord. When you reflect on how He has enabled you in the past to strengthen your interpersonal relationship skills, trusting Him with the challenges that face you will be easy and fulfilling. He can enable you to do what you can't do by yourself to nurture a secure setting for effectiveness in the ministry to which He has called you.

To God be the glory.

Notes

Introduction

1. Matthew 22:37-39.

2. 1 John 4:18.

Chapter 1

1. Genesis 1:27.

2. Clifton J. Allen, ed., *The Broadman Bible Commentary*, vol. 2 (Nashville: Broadman Press, 1970), 52.

3. Ibid., 186.

4. Thomas Welby Bozeman, "A Psychological Study of Self-Esteem from a Pastoral Frame of Reference" (Th.D. diss., New Orleans Baptist Theological Seminary, 1972), 7.

5. George Arthur Buttrick, ed., *The Interpreter's Bible*, vol. 4 (New York: Abingdon Press, 1955), 51-52.

6. Bozeman, "A Psychological Study," 7.

7. Psalms 22:20 and 35:17.

8. Harold L. Rutledge, "Personality Development," class lecture, New Orleans Baptist Theological Seminary, New Orleans, Louisiana, September 1971.

9. Matthew 22:35-40; Luke 10:25-28.

10. Bozeman, "A Psychological Study," 7.

11. Clifton J. Allen, ed., *The Broadman Commentary*, vol. 8 (Nashville: Broadman Press, 1969), 210.

12. Bozeman, "A Psychological Study," 7.

13. Ibid.

14. Paul Ramsey, *Basic Christian Ethics* (New York: Charles Scribner's Sons, 1950), 100.

15. Bozeman, "A Psychological Study," 8.

16. Nathaniel Branden, *The Psychology of Self-Esteem* (Los Angeles: Nash Publishing Corp., 1969), viii.

17. Alfred Adler, *Understanding Human Nature,* trans. Walter Beran Wolfe (London: George Allen Unwin, Ltd., 1928), 71-75.

18. Alfred Adler, *Superiority and Social Interest: A Collection of Later Writings,* ed. Heinz L. Ansbacher and Rowena R. Ansbacher (Evanston, IL: Northwestern University Press, 1964), 15.

19. Karen Horney, *Our Inner Conflicts* (New York: W. W. Norton and Company, Inc., 1945), 108-12.

20. Calvin S. Hall and Gardner Lindzey, *Theories of Personality* (New York: Libra Publishers, Inc., 1967), 133.

21. Bozeman, "A Psychological Study," 13.

22. Ibid., 14.

23. Erick Fromm, *The Art of Loving* (New York: Harper and Row, 1956), 56.

24. Ibid., 60-61.

25. Carl R. Rogers, *On Becoming a Person* (Boston: Houghton Mifflin, 1961), 34.

26. A. H. Maslow, *Motivation and Personality* (New York: Harper and Brothers, 1954), 90-91.

27. Sidney M. Jourard, *The Transparent Self* (Princeton, NJ: The D. Van Nostrand Company, Inc., 1964), 24-25.

28. James C. Diggory, *Self-Evaluation: Concepts and Studies* (New York: John Wiley and Sons Inc., 1966), 61.

29. Bozeman, "A Psychological Study," 21.

30. Ibid., 23.

31. Stanley Coopersmith, *The Antecedents of Self Esteem* (San Francisco: W. H. Freeman and Company, 1967), 164-234.

32. Ibid., 166.

33. Ibid., 185-86.

34. Anne Hitchcock Gilliland, *Understanding Preschoolers* (Nashville: Convention Press, 1969), 21.

35. Ashley Montagu, *Touching: The Human Significance of Skin* (New York: Columbia University Press, 1971), 121.

36. Bozeman, "A Psychological Study," 31.

37. Ibid., 33.

38. Ibid., 30-38.

39. Coopersmith, *Antecedents,* 19.

40. Bozeman, "A Psychological Study," 52-53.

41. Coopersmith, *Antecedents,* 19-44, 242-63.

42. Thomas Welby Bozeman, interview by author, 11 July 2002, New Orleans.

Chapter 2

1. Howard Clinebell and Charlotte Clinebell, *The Intimate Marriage* (New York: Harper and Row Publishers, 1967), 25.

2. David Mace and Vera Mace, *We Can Have Better Marriages If We Really Want Them* (Nashville: Abingdon Press, 1974), 161.

3. Joseph F. Perez, *Family Counseling: Theory and Practice* (New York: D. Van Nostrand Co., 1979), 42.

4. Virginia Satir, *Peoplemaking* (Palo Alto, CA: Science and Behavior Books, 1972), 30.

5. Reuel Howe, *The Miracle of Dialogue* (New York: Seabury Press, 1963), 50.

6. William J. Lederer and Don I. Jackson, *The Mirages of Marriage* (New York: W. W. Norton and Co., 1968), 188.

7. Irene Goldenberg and Herbert P. Goldenberg, *Family Therapy: An Overview* (Monterey, CA: Brooks/Cole Publishing Co., 1980), 37

8. Satir, *Peoplemaking,* 113.

9. Howe, *The Miracle of Dialogue,* 30.

10. Ibid., 31.

11. Clinebell and Clinebell, *The Intimate Marriage,* 20-25.

12. Cecil G. Osborne, *The Art of Understanding Your Mate* (Grand Rapids, MI: Zondervan Publishing House, 1970), 75-76.

13. L. Richard Lessor, *Love and Marriage and Trading Stamps* (Niler, IN: Argus Communications, 1971), 69.

14. Gerald D. Erickson and Terrence P. Hogan, eds., *Family Therapy: An Introduction to Theory and Technique* (Monterey, CA: Brooks/Cole Publishing Co., 1980), 129.

15. John W. Drakeford, *The Awesome Power of the Listening Ear* (Waco, TX: Word Books, 1967), 98.

16. Paul Tournier, *To Understand Each Other* (Richmond, VA: John Knox Press, 1962), 29.

17. Nena O'Neill and George O'Neill, *Open Marriage* (New York: Avon Books, 1972), 105.

18. Virginia Satir and E. L. Shostrom, *Target Five* (Santa Ana, CA: Psychological Films, 1969), videocassette.

19. Virginia Satir, *Avanta's Process,* Community II Summer Institute, 1982.

20. Satir, *Peoplemaking,* 70.

21. Ibid., 74-78.

Chapter 3

1. David Augsburger, *Care Enough to Hear and Be Heard* (Ventura, CA: Regal Books, 1982), 29.

2. Robert Fisher, *Quick to Listen, Slow to Speak* (Wheaton, IL: Tyndale House, 1987), 19-22.

3. John W. Drakeford, *The Awesome Power of the Listening Heart* (Grand Rapids, MI: Zondervan, 1982), 15.

4. Clifton Fadiman and Andre Bernard, gen. eds., *Bartlett's Book of Anecdotes* (Boston: Little, Brown & Co., 2000), 169.

5. Wayne E. Oates, *Nurturing Silence in a Noisy Heart* (Garden City, NY: Doubleday & Co., 1979), 3.

6. Leslie D. Weatherhead, *The Significance of Silence* (New York: Abingdon-Cokesbury Press, 1945), 23.

7. Drakeford, *The Awesome Power of the Listening Heart,* 155-56.

Chapter 4

1. Luke 2:41-51.

2. John 8:1-11.

3. John 19:1-16.

4. Robert Bolton, *People Skills* (New York: Simon and Schuster, 1979), 12.

5. Robert Alberti and Michael Emmons, *Your Perfect Right* (San Luis Obispo, CA: Impact Publishers, 1995), 49.

6. Ibid.

7. Arthur J. Lange and Patricia Jakubowski, *Responsible Assertive Behavior* (Champaign, IL: Research Press, 1976), 9.

8. Ibid.

9. Bolton, *People Skills,* 124.

10. Ibid.

11. Ibid., 129-30.

12. Ibid., 130-31.

13. Lange and Jakubowski, *Responsible Assertive Behavior,* 21-26.

14. *Webster's Tenth New Collegiate Dictionary* (2001), s.v. "Aggression."

15. Bolton, *People Skills,* 124.

16. Alberti and Emmons, *Your Perfect Right,* 50.

17. Lange and Jakubowski, *Responsible Assertive Behavior,* 10.

18. Alberti and Emmons, *Your Perfect Right,* 50.

19. Lange and Jakubowski, *Responsible Assertive Behavior,* 132.

20. Ibid.

21. Ibid., 28-30.

22. Ibid., 7.

23. Alberti and Emmons, *Your Perfect Right*, 57.

24. Bolton, *People Skills*, 136.

25. Alberti and Emmons, *Your Perfect Right*, 109-13.

26. "Assertiveness Training," *Assertiveness Training—Psychological Self-Help*; available from the internet at http://mentalhelp.net/psyhelp/chap13/chap13e.htm; accessed on 2 July 2002.

Chapter 5

1. 2 Corinthians 2:9.

2. Matthew 18:21.

3. 2 Corinthians 2:9.

4. Ibid.

5. Luke 7:47.

6. 2 Corinthians 2:11.

Chapter 6

1. Luke 15:17-24.

2. Psalm 46:10.

3. Frederick A. DiBlasio of the University of Maryland School of Social Work has written several articles defining and emphasizing the volitional aspect of forgiveness. Some of the ideas presented here are based on his work.

4. Ephesians 4:26.

Chapter 7

1. Exodus 34:7.

2. John 13:34; John 15:12, 17.

3. 2 Corinthians 5:17.

Chapter 8

1. See Myron C. Madden, *The Power to Bless* (New Orleans: Insight Press, 1999).

2. Matthew 22:36-40; Mark 12:28-31.

3. Matthew 28:19-20; Mark 16:15-18.

4. Genesis 27-48.

5. Mark 10:13-16.

6. Luke 18:15-17.

7. Matthew 19:13-15.

8. 1 John 2:1.

9. Romans 8:16-17.

10. Acts 9:1-22.

Chapter 9

1. "Amazing Grace," words by John Newton (1725-1807), early American melody.

Chapter 10

1. Matthew 6:19-20.

Chapter 11

1. *Merriam-Webster's Collegiate Dictionary,* 10th ed., s.v. "Etiquette."

2. *Encarta World English Dictionary,* North American ed., Microsoft Corporation, 2001.

3. Sue Fox, *Etiquette for Dummies* (Foster City, CA: IDG Books Worldwide, Inc., 1999), 2

4. Proverbs 31:10-31.

5. 1 Peter 4.9

6. Luke 19:1-10; 10:38-42.

7. Romans 12:13.

8. Bradley Chance, "Fellowship," *Holman Bible Dictionary,* ed. Trent C. Butler (Nashville: Holman Bible Publishers, 1991).

Chapter 12

1. Genesis 2:18, 20.

2. J. Clark Hensley, *Good News for Today's Singles* (Nashville: Convention Press, 1985), 35.

3. John R. Landgraf, *Singling, A New Way to Live the Single Life* (Louisville: Westminster/John Knox Press, 1990), 18.

4. Ibid.

5. "Love on the Rocks: Taking Aim at Divorce Rates," *Trend Letter,* vol. 21, no. 8 (15 April 2002).

6. John 13:34.

7. Hensley, *Good News for Today's Singles,* 30-31.

8. Genesis 1:3-5.

9. John 10:10.

10. Genesis 1:26-27.

11. Hebrews 12:1-2.

Chapter 14

1. Hendrie Weisinger, *Emotional Intelligence at Work* (San Francisco: Jossey-Bass, 1998), xvii.

2. Daniel Goleman, *Emotional Intelligence: Why It Can Matter More Than IQ* (New York: Bantam Books, 1995), 41-42.

3. Ibid., 43.

4. Cheryl Hamilton and Cordell Parker, *Communicating for Results: A Guide for Business and the Professions,* 5th ed. (Belmont, CA: Wadsworth Publishing Company, 1997), 65.

5. Goleman, *Emotional Intelligence,* 43.

6. John 15:8-11, 13.

7. Hebrews 4:12.

8. Goleman, *Emotional Intelligence,* 43.

9. Ephesians 4:26.

10. Goleman, *Emotional Intelligence,* 88.

11. Galatians 6:9.

12. Romans 12:15.

13. Matthew 22:37.

14. Matthew 22:39.

15. Hamilton and Parker, *Communicating for Results,* 11.

16. James 1:19.

17. Proverbs 20:5.

18. Eugene Peterson, *The Contemplative Pastor* (Grand Rapids, MI: Eerdmans Publishing Co., 1989), 115.

19. Genesis 1:26-27.

20. 1 Corinthians 12:4.

21. *DISC Personal Profile System* (Minneapolis: Carlson Learning Company).

22. Weisinger, *Emotional Intelligence at Work,* 1.

23. 2 Corinthians 5:17.

24. Galatians 5:22-23.

Chapter 15

1. Robert M. Bramson, *Coping with Difficult People* (New York: Dell Publishing, 1981), 13-14.

2. Rick Brinkman and Rick Kirschner, *Dealing with People You Can't Stand* (New York: McGraw-Hill, Inc., 1994), 84.

3. Ibid., 5.

4. Bramson, *Coping,* 29-30.

5. Brinkman and Kirschner, *Dealing,* 90.

6. Ibid., 95-104.

7. Ibid., 98-99.

8. Ibid., 7.

9. Bramson, *Coping,* 85-97.

10. Ibid., 138-57.

11. Ibid.

12. Ibid., 43-68.

13. Ibid., 59-68.

14. Ibid., 100-111.

15. Ibid.

16. Brinkman and Kirschner, *Dealing,* 161-70.

17. Bramson, *Coping,* 69.

18. Paul Meier, *Don't Let the Jerks Get the Best of You* (Nashville: Thomas Nelson Publishers, 1993), 6-7.

19. Ibid.

20. Psalm 139:23-24.

21. Bramson, *Coping,* 170.

Chapter 16

1. Edward G. Dobson, Speed B. Leas, and Marshall Shelley, *Mastering Conflict and Controversy* (Portland: Multnomah, 1992), 83-94.

2. John 17:23.

3. Gerald L. Borchert, *John 12-21,* The New American Commentary, ed. E. Ray Clendenen, vol. 25b (Nashville: Broadman and Holman Publishers, 2002), 206-7.

4. James Kouzes and Barry Posner, *Credibility: How Leaders Gain and Lose It, Why People Demand It* (San Francisco: Jossey-Bass, 1993), 14.

5. Proverbs 29:18.

6. Samuel P. Tragelles, *Gesenius' Hebrew and Chaldee Lexicon to the Old Testament Scriptures* (Grand Rapids, MI: Wm. B. Eerdmans Publishing Company, 1974), 269.

7. Marshall Shelley, *Well-Intentioned Dragons: Ministering to Problem People in the Church* (Waco, TX: Word Books, 1985), 85-87.

8. W. A. Criswell, *Criswell's Guidebook for Pastors* (Nashville: Broadman Press, 1980), 88.

9. Matthew 9:17.

10. Proverbs 11:14.

11. John C. Maxwell, *Developing the Leader Within You* (Nashville: Thomas Nelson Publishers, 1993), 75-76.

12. Matthew 5:23-24.

13. Matthew 5:44.

14. Proverbs 15:1.

15. Ephesians 4:15.

Chapter 17

1. Matthew 28:18-20.

2. Colossians 4:6.

3. Matthew 7:12.

4. Acts 15:36-40; 2 Timothy 4:11.

5. Joseph Luft, *Group Processes: An Introduction to Group Dynamics* (Palo Alto, CA: National Press Books, 1963), 10-12.

6. Exodus 4:10-12.

7. 1 Samuel 16:11-13.

8. Acts 22:6-16.

9. 2 Timothy 1:3-14.

10. John 15:15.

11. Matthew 12:46-50.

12. Psalm 133:1.

Chapter 18

1. Titus 2:2-6.

2. 2 Corinthians 5:18, 19.

3. 2 Corinthians 12:9.

4. 1 Corinthians 12:12.

5. Colossians 1:18.

Chapter 19

1. 2 Thessalonians 3:10.

2. More information can be received about The Greenleaf Center for Servant Leadership at http://www.greenleaf.org.

3. John 2:15.

4. Matthew 12:13; Mark 11:17; Luke 19:46.

5. Luke 8:1.

6. Mark 2:14-17.

7. Mark 10:13-16.

8. John 4:1-42.

9. John 2:1-11.

10. Matthew 17:1-8; Luke 9:28-36.

11. Luke 10:29-37.

12. Luke 2:41-50.

13. Luke 2:52.

14. Acts 10:38.

15. Harold L. Rutledge, notes and handout from the course Crisis Counseling, New Orleans Baptist Theological Seminary, March 1974.

Chapter 20

1. Robert L. Barker, *The Social Work Dictionary*, 4th ed. (Washington, DC: National Association of Social Workers, 1999), 325.

2. Naomi I. Brill, *Working with People: The Helping Process*, 6th ed. (New York: Longman, 1998), 150.

3. Ibid., 149.

4. Ibid.

5. Marion Bilich, Susan Bonfiglio, and Steven Carlson, *Shared Grace: Therapists and Clergy Working Together* (New York: The Haworth Pastoral Press, 2000), 131-33.

6. Ibid.

Chapter 21

1. John Homer Miller, *Take a Look at Yourself* (New York: Abingdon-Cokesbury Press, 1943), 93.

2. Vance Havner, *Moments of Decision* (Grand Rapids, MI: Baker Book House, 1979), 7.

3. Genesis 3:1-16.

4. Hebrews 11:8-10.

5. Ibid., 16.

6. Genesis 13:1-13.

7. Hebrews 11:24-26.

8. Joshua 24:15.

9. 2 Samuel 11:1-27.

10. Esther 4:15-16.

11. John 18:15-27.

12. Ruth 1:15-17.

13. Matthew 26:14-16.

14. John 10:7-18.

15. Theodore Isaac Rubin, *Overcoming Indecisiveness: The Eight Stages of Effective Decisionmaking* (New York: Avon Books, 1985), 12-17.

16. Ibid., 10.

17. Ibid.

18. Romans 6:15-23.

19. Laurie Beth Jones, *The Path* (New York: Hyperion, 1996), xvii.

20. Rubin, *Overcoming*, 144.

21. Ibid.

22. T. B. Maston, *Right or Wrong* (Nashville: Broadman Press, 1955), 3.

23. Ibid., 4-9.

24. Ibid., 29-33.

25. Ibid., 35-39.

26. Ibid., 41-46.

Chapter 22

1. Acts 20:35.

2. Matthew 22:39.

Recommended Reading

Alberti, Robert, and Michael Emmons. *Your Perfect Right*. San Luis Obispo, CA: Impact Publishers, 1995.

Allen, Tom. *Congregations in Conflict*. Camp Hill, PA: Christian Publications, 1991.

Augsburger, David. *Care Enough to Hear and Be Heard*. Ventura, CA: Regal Books, 1982.

_____. *Caring Enough to Confront*. Ventura, CA: Regal Books, 1973.

Bagby, Daniel. *Understanding Anger in the Church*. Nashville: Broadman, 1979.

Barker, Robert L. *The Social Work Dictionary*, 4th ed. Washington, DC: National Association of Social Workers Press, 1999.

Bilich, Marion, Susan Bonfiglio, and Steven Carlson. *Shared Grace: Therapists and Clergy Working Together*. New York: The Haworth Pastoral Press, 2000.

Bisagno, John R. *Letters to Timothy: A Handbook for Pastors*. Nashville: Broadman and Holman Publishers, 2001.

Bolton, Robert. *People Skills*. New York: Simon and Schuster, 1986.

Bramson, Robert M. *Coping with Difficult People*. New York: Dell Publishing, 1981.

Branden, Nathaniel. *The Power of Self Esteem*. Deerfield Beach, FL: Health Communications, Inc., 1992.

Bratcher, Edward B. *The Walk on Water Syndrome.* Waco, TX: Word Books, 1994.

Bridges, Jerry. *Trusting God Even When Life Hurts.* Colorado Springs: NavPress, 1993, c 1988.

Brill, Naomi I. *Working with People: The Helping Process,* 6th ed. Longman: New York, 1998.

Brinkman, Rick, and Rick Kirschner. *Dealing with People You Can't Stand.* New York: McGraw-Hill, Inc., 1994.

Campbell, Barry, ed. *Toolbox for [Busy] Pastors.* Nashville: Convention Press, 1998.

Carlin, Lesley, and Honore McDonough Ervin. *Things You Need to Be Told: A Handbook for Polite Behavior in a Tacky, Rude World!* New York: Berkeley Books, 2001.

Chance, Bradley. "Fellowship." *Holman Bible Dictionary.* Edited by Trent C. Butler. Nashville: Holman Bible Publishers, 1991.

Chandler, Charles. *Minister's Support Group: Alternative to Burnout.* Nashville: Convention Press, 1987.

Clairmont, Patsy. *Normal Is Just a Setting on Your Dryer.* Colorado Springs: Focus on the Family Publishing, 1993.

Clowse, Barbara Barksdale. *Women, Decision Making and the Future.* Atlanta: John Knox Press, 1987.

Cothen, Joe H. *Equipped for Good Work: A Guide for Pastors.* 2d ed. Revised by Joe H. Cothen and Jerry N. Barlow. Gretna, LA: Pelican Publishing Company, 2002.

Crabb, Larry. *Inside Out.* Colorado Springs: NavPress, 1988.

Criswell, W. A. *Criswell's Guidebook for Pastors.* Nashville: Broadman Press, 1980.

Damon, Roberta McBride. *Relationship Skills.* Birmingham, AL: Woman's Missionary Union, SBC, 1993.

Diehm, William J. *Sharpening Your People Skills: 10 Tools for Success in Any Relationship.* Nashville: Broadman & Holman Publishers, 1996.

Dobson, Edward G., Speed B. Leas, and Marshall Shelley. *Mastering Conflict and Controversy*. Portland: Multnomah, 1992.

Drakeford, John W. *The Awesome Power of the Listening Ear*. Waco, TX: Word Books, 1967.

_____. *The Awesome Power of the Listening Heart*. Grand Rapids, MI: Zondervan, 1982.

Dresser, Norine. *Multicultural Manners: New Rules of Etiquette for a Changing Society*. New York: Wiley & Sons, 1996.

Egan, Gerald. *The Skilled Helper*. Pacific Grove, CA: Brooks/Cole Publishing Company, 1994.

Engstrom, Ted. *Integrity*. Waco, TX: Word, 1987.

Fehr, Beverly Anne. *Friendship Processes*. Thousand Oaks, CA: Sage Publications, 1996.

Fisher, B. Aubrey, and Katherine L. Adams. *Interpersonal Communication: Pragmatics of Human Relationships*. New York: McGraw Hill, Inc., 1994.

Forni, P. M. *Choosing Civility: The 25 Rules of Considerate Conduct*. New York: St. Martin's Press, 2002.

Fox, Sue. *Etiquette for Dummies*. Foster City, CA: IDG Books Worldwide, Inc., 1999.

Gangel, Kenneth O., and Samuel L. Canine. *Communication and Conflict Management in Churches and Christian Organizations*. Nashville: Broadman Press, 1992.

Glass, Lillian. *Toxic People: 10 Ways of Dealing with People Who Make Your Life Miserable*. New York: St. Martin's Press, 1997.

Goleman, Daniel. *Emotional Intelligence: Why It Can Matter More Than IQ*. New York: Bantam Books, 1995.

Grant-Sokolosky, Valerie. *The Little Instruction Book of Business Etiquette*. Tulsa, OK: TradeLife Books, 1998.

Halverstadt, Hugh F. *Managing Church Conflict*. Louisville, KY: Westminster/John Knox Press, 1991.

Hansel, Tim. *When I Relax I Feel Guilty*. Elgin, IL: David C. Cook Publishing Co., 1979.

Hartley, Fred. *The Teenage Book of Manners—Please!* Westwood, NJ: Barbour Books, 1991.

Havner, Vance. *Moments of Decision.* Grand Rapids, MI: Baker Book House, 1979.

Hensley, J. Clark. *Good News for Today's Singles.* Nashville: Convention Press, 1985.

Hester, Dennis J. *Pastor, We Need to Talk!* Shelby, NC: His Way Publishing, 2001.

Hocker, Joyce L., and William W. Wilmot. *Interpersonal Conflict.* New York: William C. Brown Publishers, 1991.

Hull, Bill. *The Disciple-Making Pastor.* Old Tappan, NJ: Revell, 1988.

Hybels, Bill. *Who You Are When No One's Looking.* Downers Grove, IL: InterVarsity, 1987.

Jones, Laurie Beth. *The Path.* New York: Hyperion, 1996.

Kaplan, Burton. *Winning People Over: 14 Days to Power and Confidence.* Paramus, NJ: Prentice Hall, 1996.

Kennedy, Gerald. *With Singleness of Heart.* New York: Harper and Brothers, 1951.

Kouzes, James, and Barry Posner. *Credibility: How Leaders Gain and Lose It, Why People Demand It.* San Francisco: Jossey-Bass, 1993.

Landgraf, John R. *Singling, A New Way to Live the Single Life.* Louisville, KY: Westminster/John Knox Press, 1990.

Lange, Arthur J. and Patricia Jakubowski, *Responsible Assertive Behavior.* Champaign, IL: Research Press, 1976.

Law, William. *A Serious Call to a Devout and Holy Life.* Wilton, CT: Morehouse-Barlow, 1982.

Malony, H. Newton. *Win-Win Relationships.* Nashville: Broadman & Holman Publishers, 1995.

Martin, Judith. *Miss Manners' Basic Training.* New York: Crown Publishers, 1997.

_____. *Miss Manners' Guide for the Turn of the Millennium.* New York: Simon and Schuster Inc., 1989.

Maslow, A. H. *Motivation and Personality*. New York: Harper and Brothers, 1954.

Maston, T. B. *Right or Wrong*. Nashville: Broadman Press, 1955.

Maxwell, John C. *Be a People Person*. Wheaton, IL: Victor Books, 1989.

——————. *Developing the Leader within You*. Nashville: Thomas Nelson Publishers, 1993.

——————. *Developing the Leaders around You*. Nashville: Thomas Nelson, Inc., 1995.

McGinnis, Alan Loy. *Bringing Out the Best in People*. Minneapolis: Augsbury Publishing House, 1985.

Meier, Paul. *Don't Let Jerks Get the Best of You*. Nashville: Thomas Nelson Publishers, 1993.

Merrill, David W., and Roger H. Reid. *Personal Styles and Effective Performance: Make Your Style Work for You*. Radnor, PA: Chilton Book Co., 1983.

Miller, J. Keith. *A Hunger for Healing: The Twelve Steps as a Classic Model for Christian Spiritual Growth*. San Francisco: HarperSanFrancisco, 1991.

Miller, John Homer. *Take a Look at Yourself*. New York: Abingdon-Cokesbury Press, 1943.

Miller, Sherod, Daniel B. Wackman, Elam Nunnally, and Phyllis A. Miller. *Connecting with Self and Others*. Littleton, CO: Interpersonal Communication Programs, Inc., 1988.

Minirth, Frank B., and Paul D. Meier. *Happiness Is a Choice*. Grand Rapids, MI: Baker Book House, 1978.

Mitchell, Mary, and John Corr. *The Complete Idiot's Guide to Etiquette*. Indianapolis: Alpha Books, 2000.

Moore, June Hines. *The Etiquette Advantage: Rules for the Professional*. Nashville: Broadman & Holman, 1998.

——————. *You Can Raise a Well-Mannered Child*. Nashville: Broadman & Holman, 1996.

Morton, Thomas. *Life and Holiness*. New York: Image, 1963.

O'Connor, Elizabeth. *Journey Inward, Journey Outward.* New York: Harper & Row Publishers, 1968.

Perrot, Les. *High Maintenance Relationships.* Wheaton, IL: Tyndale House, 1989.

Peterson, Eugene. *The Contemplative Pastor.* Grand Rapids, MI: Eerdmans Publishing Co., 1989.

_____. *Working the Angles.* Grand Rapids, MI: Eerdmans Publishing Co., 1987.

Platz, Ann, and Susan Wales. *Social Graces.* Eugene, OR: Harvest House Publishers, 1999.

Post, Elizabeth L. *Emily Post's Advice for Every Dining Occasion.* New York: HarperCollins Publishers, 1994.

Post, Peggy. *Emily Post's Etiquette.* New York: HarperCollins Publishers, 1997.

Radcliffe, Robert J. *Effective Ministry as an Associate Pastor.* Grand Rapids, MI: Kregel Publications, 1998.

Rhodes, Roy G. *Fly with Eagles: The Business of Winning.* Dallas: Rhodes Publishing Company, 1991.

Rollins, Catherine E. *52 Ways to Build Your Self Esteem and Confidence.* Nashville: Thomas Nelson Publishers, 1992.

Rubin, Theodore Issac. *Overcoming Indecisiveness: The Eight Stages of Effective Decisionmaking.* New York: Avon Books, 1985.

Sanford, John A. *Between People.* Mahwah, NJ: Paulist Press, 1988.

Satir, Virginia. *Making Contact.* Berkeley, CA: Celestial Arts, 1976.

_____. *Peoplemaking.* Palo Alto, CA: Science and Behavior Books, 1972.

_____. *Self Esteem.* Millbrae, CA: Celestial Arts, 1975.

Schooley, Shirley. *Conflict Management.* Birmingham, AL: New Hope, 1994.

Segaloff, Nat. *The Everything Etiquette Mini Book.* Holbrook, MA: Adams Media Corporation, 2001.

Sehnert, Keith W. *Stress/Unstress.* Minneapolis: Augsburg Publishing House, 1981.

Shaughnessy, Diane. *Let's Talk about Good Manners.* New York: Powerkids Press, 1997.

Shelley, Marshall. *Well-Intentioned Dragon: Ministering to Problem People in the Church.* Waco, TX: Word Books, 1985.

Smedes, Lewis B. *Caring and Commitment.* New York: HarperCollins, 1988.

Sphar, Asa, and Argile Smith. *Helping Hurting People: A Handbook on Reconciliation-Focused Counseling and Preaching.* Lanham, MD: University Press of America, 2003.

Stevens, Paul. *Balancing Your Life: Setting Personal Goals.* San Jose, CA: Resource Publishing, 1996.

Stewart, Marjabella Young. *The New Etiquette: Real Manners for Real People in Real Situations—An A-to-Z Guide.* New York: St. Martin's Griffin, 1997.

Tingley, Judith C. *Genderflex: Men and Women Speaking the Same Language at Work.* New York: American Management Association, 1993.